THE LOVE OF GOALKEEPING

MANY SPORTS, ONE LOVE...

TOMAŽ LAŠIČ

First edition, 2020

ISBN: 978-0-6489398-0-1 (paperback)

ISBN: 978-0-6489398-1-8 (eBook)

Illustrations by Sebastian Lasic

Published by Tomaž Lašič

Email: tomaz@theloveofgoalkeeping.net

www.theloveofgoalkeeping.net

NATIONAL
LIBRARY
OF AUSTRALIA

A catalogue record for this work is available from the National Library of Australia

To goalkeepers and all who care about them.

First impressions of the book ...

"This important book warns and informs how important the last line of defence is in water polo and any other sport and how much there can be learned from different sports. In analysing developments of sport, it is very clear that the role of the goal-keeper is becoming an increasingly decisive factor of success.

I recommend this unique book to both those seeking the competitive edge or anyone just interested in better understanding goalkeeping and goalkeepers in any sport. The passion for goalkeeping shines through!"

Ratko Rudić,
4 x Olympic Champion water polo coach,
ISHOF Hall of Fame

"There are a number of books which discuss the role of the goalkeeper from one specific sport's perspective. 'The Love of Goalkeeping' is a brilliantly written and unique book that connects perspectives and explores the many similarities of the goalkeeping position within a variety of sports."

Dave Whalley,
Blackburn Rovers FC, Inglewood FC,
DWG Football Goalkeeping

"I have always preferred to save a goal rather than score one. Your book gives me hope that my dreams and goals can be nurtured and that I can continue to learn from all sports."

Cooper Dobson,
water polo junior goalkeeper

"As a mother of a 15 year old, I've realised that I can't influence his choice in being a goalkeeper as opposed to a field player. Thank you Tomaz, your book has given me insight into his need to identify as a goalkeeper and the story he wants to write."

Daele Dobson,
mother

"Every lay person or a professional coach alike can find in this book things to help them understand how and why the position of a goalkeeper is so unique and important. The book has opened some new perspectives even to me as an elite goalkeeping coach and I will definitely use them in my work with goalkeepers.

In short - this very readable book is an ideal mix of experience, knowledge and above all the love of working with and understanding goalkeepers."

Aljaž Pavlič,
EHF Master Handball Coach

"Everything written in this book is without doubt relatable to the ongoing challenges of coaching the next generations of goalkeepers. It's a fascinating position with so many components to bring together and assist in performance when it all matters - game day!

I have also been delving deeper into the position and hoping to come up with some more finite equations that may help the goalkeeper of the future. It has become a very intellectual position as it has evolved with the game over the years. Human traits, patterns of behaviours and breaking the cycle of bad habits to form new ideas to allow them to grow and flourish. How goalkeepers play and train now is very different to the traditional days. But there is room for both (then and now) in my opinion. Let's learn, together!"

Danny Milosevic,
Socceroos, Leeds United FC, Perth Glory FC

"This book gives you an understanding of how the mind and body of a goalkeeper work and explains how important the role it is in any sport. It reminds you how goalkeepers have to work not just on their skill but also their mindset, ability, communication, leadership and most importantly, their presence in goal. After reading this book, you will have a greater appreciation of who the people on the last line of defence are.

I think this book will inspire a lot of up and coming keepers to improve their craft, current ones to keep at it and past keepers may come back to it in some capacity."

Abdul-Raouf Mohamed-Isa,
futsal goalkeeper

"A few years ago at an international water polo coaches conference, we collectively wrestled with the equation Goalkeeper + Players = Team. In my view, the numbers we came up with say it all about the importance of goalkeepers: Goalkeeper (50%) + Players (50%) = Team (100%).

Goalkeepers may be 'weirdos' as the quoted poet in this book lovingly calls them, but they need a lot of work with and necessary attention. From this point of view, this is a very valuable book. As the title suggests and the contents confirm, the book demonstrates not only a significant investment of knowledge, time and experience put into it but the love that was written with. Congratulations and thank you!"

Dr Igor Štirn,
University of Ljubljana - Faculty of Sport

"Loved every word!"

Danielle Woodhouse,
Olympic water polo gold medal goalkeeper

Contents

Acknowledgements xi

Foreword xv

1   Introduction..1

2   The role and importance of a goalkeeper............................7

3   Moving like a cat...21

4   Reading the game 35

5   Fit and able 53

6   Inside goalkeeper's head...71

7   The Presence 91

8   Idols and role models...105

9   Teaching and learning the craft 119

10 Finding and selecting a goalkeeper.................................135

11 Summary...153

Next step..171

About the author 173

Notes 175

Acknowledgements

To make this book authentic, I heard from, spoke with and otherwise engaged with over a hundred goalkeepers, coaches, administrators and even parents of goalkeepers from different sports, different countries, different ages and different levels of experience. To all of you in the list below and to many others who preferred not to have their name published - a heartfelt *'thank you'*, in more than a dozen native languages you speak!

Abdul-Raouf Mohamed-Isa, Alan Borg Cole, Alex Dunn,
Aljaž Pavlič, Akos Biró, Andras Gyori, Anna Torres,
Anton Lašič, Antun Novosel, Benjamin Teraš, Biljana Lakić,
Bogdan Jianu, Brian Stubbs, Brice Latour,
Chaouachi Mohamed, Christos Mylonakis, Cooper Dobson,
Daele Dobson, Dan Hennessy, Danielle Woodhouse,
Dave Whalley, Davorin Taubek Golubić, Eamonn Armitage,
Erika Wenzel, Faizal Alwadi, Frederic Houdelet,
Fredi Radojković, Georgina Kovacs-Muller, Gerald Pecqueur,
Gilly Johnson, Glenn Townsend, Hendrik Hummel,
Igor Štirn, Jean Francois Pegand, John Hedges, Jure Šterbucl,
Jure Šujica, Kostas Paslis, Lilian Hedges, Liz Weekes,

Lorène Derenty, Lorenzo Cenci, Luka Stanič, Marco Rossi,
Mark Klarič, Mark McNamara, Marko Prcać, Marko Žagar,
Marta Bon, Matic Škrjanec, Maurizio Cavallini,
Michael Zellmer, Milan de Koff, Miša Marinček Ribežl,
Nikola Rajlić, Olivier Aula, Olivier Carrez, Patrice Vanhoute,
Philippe Loriot, Pierre Gautier, Ratko Rudić,
Riccardo Carraro, Richard Charlesworth, Rob Caruso,
Robert Beguš, Robert Sappé, Ron Morelli, Russell McKinnon,
Sean Reid, Serena Getty, Shayan Ghasemidaryan,
Slavko Stržinar, Stefani Jelić, Stephane Hennicaux,
Thierry Desnoulet, Thomas Freeman, Thomas Rodrigues,
Tibor Seress, Tomaž Tomšič, Urh Brana, Vitalyi Dobrov,
Vjekoslav Kobešćak, William Mather, Wim Schoeman
and Zoran Kačić

Apart from this wonderful group of contributors, there are
certain people without whose time, effort and care this book
would absolutely not be in front of you today. I would like to
acknowledge and sincerely thank Georgina Kovacs-Muller,
Head Coach of Womens Water Polo programme at the Western
Australian Institute of Sport, Dave Whalley, the immensely experienced principal coach at Dave Whalley Football Goalkeeping,
and Zoran Kačić, the legendary Croatian goalkeeper, Olympic
level coach and publisher of several books on goalkeeping, for
their invaluable critical chapter reads, comments, suggestions,
conversations and encouragement all along.

As I finished the book, I gave it to many people to read and
offer their honest views. Thank you all who have taken the time,

some true legends of sport and beyond among you. I feel deeply grateful and privileged to have had Ric Charlesworth, the legendary dual Olympic gold medal coach of the Australian field hockey teams, coaching mentor, writer and consultant write not only a brief review but the entire foreword to the book. The book itself was skilfully turned from a manuscript into a well designed publication by the wonderful Rommie Corso of Hardshell Publishing.

Enormous gratitude also goes to my wife Anna and sons Sebastian and Toby for their constructive critique, support, putting up with my early mornings, late nights and absent mindedness for hundreds of hours while this book was being born. Speaking of family and gratitude, the beautiful minimalist illustrations that try to capture the essence of each chapter and incorporate many different sports with a goalkeeper are the work of Sebastian, a budding graphic media designer.

Foreword

I have long believed the goalkeeper is the most important player in the team. Especially in games where scoring is low, the goalkeeper's influence on the result is seminal. Accordingly, coaches should make sure they provide goalkeepers with the attention they require. Sadly, I have often observed this is not so and the goalkeeper can be unloved and neglected.

This occurs often because coaches, whether experienced or novices, do not feel confident to 'coach' goalkeeping. This book provides advice and ideas that should help all coaches expand their goalkeeping knowledge and find a way to do justice to the goalkeepers in their teams.

Tomaz's understanding of what great goalkeeping is and what it takes to make great goalkeepers is clear. Equally, he outlines how to prepare custodians at every level of competition. He understands the movement patterns, the technical aspects, the tactical considerations and the mental and physical demands.

In field hockey I had four crucial expectations of the goalkeeper. Firstly, make sure you save all the savable shots. Secondly, control rebounds and blocks so the opposition doesn't get another chance. Thirdly, be decisive and assertive in your actions and finally, be mobile and communicate with teammates. The goalkeeper has to be a defensive organiser.

This book covers all of these matters and so much more. After the technique, tactics, movement and psychology of the custodian, it provides advice on how to project a presence, teaching methods and means and finding and selecting those that guard the net.

For me the art of selecting has always been one of the most difficult aspects of coaching. You aim to build quality, depth and create a competitive environment. This always makes for difficult selection dilemmas. The chapter on 'finding and selecting' reminded me of many of my mistakes. We once selected the goalkeeper with the best reflexes rather than the best decision maker under pressure. It did not end well!

I am reminded of the comments of Markus Weise the very successful German field hockey coach who wrote to me about his goalkeeper selection. "She contributed really a lot to our 2004 victory in Athens not only as a first-class goalie but also as a first-class personality and mentality". One must always consider the whole package and Markus outlined how the technical had to be married with the mental approach. Tomaz raises many examples of such considerations that require us to be curious and introspective.

The book contains quirky and informative illustrations which convey the messages clearly and directly. The literary, historical and contemporary references from the Greek Stoic Epictetus to Conan Doyle to Bruce Lee reinforce important messages. Additionally, the annotated index provided offers the enthusiast an opportunity to search further to increase their understanding of the science and art of goalkeeping.

No matter what your sport, this book is a beauty which can be easily read and is full of knowledge and advice. Every coach should have it on their shelf or in their laptop.

– Dr Richard Charlesworth

Ric Charlesworth is a doctor of medicine with an honorary science degree and an arts degree majoring in philosophy and history. He is a former captain of the Australian Hockey Team and the Western Australian State Hockey Team and Cricket Team. He played field hockey for Australia for a record 17 years and played first class cricket for nearly a decade.

He was elected a member of Federal parliament in 1983 and retired 10 years later. His plans to pursue medicine were diverted when he took on the position of National Coach of the Australian Women's Hockey Team from 1993 to 2000. Between 2009 and 2014 he coached the Men's team. He has authored five books on coaching and team management.

In four World Cups and three Olympic Games as coach of Australia, Charlesworth's teams won gold on six occasions and once won bronze. They won eight of nine Champions Trophy tournaments and two Commonwealth Games gold medals… a record never equaled in the sport. Between 1994 and 2014 Charlesworth was 'Coach of the Year', again unrivalled, eight times!

Given that in the last 60 years Australia has won five Hockey World Cups and four Olympic gold medals (nine in total), Charlesworth's involvement in seven of these as a coach or player is an extraordinary contribution to the sport.

'Contact' by Sebastian Lasic

1

Introduction

"Can I be a goalkeeper?"

Only a day before I asked my coach this question, I was a field player standing in for a sick goalkeeper during a tournament. In the dying seconds of the biggest and most important game in my life I saved a penalty that secured a gutsy draw against heavy favourites. I was … ten years old.

Since then, I kept goals in games and moments where not just mine but the fortunes of entire clubs and national teams hinged on my performance in front of crowds of thousands of people and TV cameras. But I *still* remember that rush that came with saving what, in the scheme of things, would have to be one of the least important penalties in the history of water polo. Since then, I *belonged* to that space in front of the goal. I wasn't just covering it, I *was* it.

After finishing playing water polo at the highest level I also stood, competitively but very amateur, in handball, futsal and football goals. A few years ago I started working with young football goalkeepers, one of them our younger son, and talking to goalkeeping specialists in that sport. All this action outside my 'native' sport increased my curiosity and a growing realisation of how much the goalkeepers and coaches working with them in different sports have in common. Football, futsal, field hockey, ice hockey, handball, lacrosse, hurling ... all these other sports with a goalkeeper! [1]

As I started to borrow training activities and principles of goalkeeping across different sports, I began to realise not only how much we have in common but also how much we could actually help and learn from each other, across the sports.

Last year, a good friend and a former champion goalkeeper suggested we promote a recently established programme for young goalkeepers with the slogan *'I am a goalkeeper. What's your superpower?'* It struck me not just as a catchy promo line but a great way to describe a goalkeeper in any sport with one. Whatever the sport, the goalkeepers need superior vision, reaction, focus, speed and anticipation. They need to be the bravest and most psychologically stable member of the team, an excellent leader, communicator and the scariest obstacle to the opposition as they hold the most trusted and responsible position on the field, and more. So, I decided to explore these 'superpowers' that we, the goalkeepers, share across various sports and organise this exploration in a book now in front of you.

The book starts with a look at the **Role and importance of a goalkeeper** through the past, present and future. The chapter also considers the difference between a person 'playing in goals' and 'being a goalkeeper' as part of one's identity. Chapter 3, *Moving like a cat*, looks at the geometry, rationalisation of movement and balance that is almost axiomatic to goalkeepers across different sports. Chapter 4, *Reading the game*, adds to this by exploring the reaction, visual tracking and decision making, complemented by goalkeepers' ability to read the play and anticipate the shots and patterns of play that makes us easily do the seemingly impossible things. Chapter 5, *Fit and able*, looks at some of the common physical attributes and abilities of goalkeepers across sports, their difference in the use of the energy systems compared to field players and common strengths such as core and agility. Chapter 6 takes a trip *Inside goalkeeper's head* to look at the focus, levels of arousal and anxiety to deal with fears of injury and failure, pressure and tendency for perfectionism as prominent impacts on goalkeepers' performance and well-being.

Chapter 7, *The Presence*, is dedicated to goalkeepers' presence that deters the opposition and inspires their team, based not only on the ability to keep the ball out of the net but also good communication and leadership. Chapter 8 explores the importance of *Idols and role models* not just in finding one but being one too. As an educator, I could not go past writing a chapter on *Teaching and learning the craft* in developing goalkeepers. Chapter 10, *Finding and selecting a goalkeeper*, looks to expand goalkeeping talent identification beyond 'happy accidents' and make picking the goalkeeper for the most limited spot in the team a little less stressful and more meaningful to both the goalkeepers and the coaches, often not goalkeepers themselves.

The key ideas from the book are wrapped up in the generously sized *Summary* chapter. The book ends with an invitation to all who care about goalkeepers to take the *Next step* and connect with each other to hopefully spark hundreds of conversations about goalkeeping not just within but across what sometimes feel like silos of our own sports.

The French have a wonderful word for the sort of thing this book is - a *bricolage*. It is a mix of popular articles, academic research, the stories of people I have engaged with in writing this book and my personal reflections and insights that cross the fields of coaching, physiology, psychology, education, sociology, history and others. I have worked in these fields not just as a water polo goalkeeper and coach but as a teacher, my primary professional field, researcher, educator, writer, teaching coach and mentor. The book is not intended as a detailed coaching manual but I sincerely hope it stimulates your thinking about understanding and working with goalkeepers whatever the sport with one.

Yes, goalkeeping is *both* a science we can test and improve, and an art form, a canvas we paint or to express ourselves on. But the love[2] for it is essential to make it work and last. Welcome to 'The Love of Goalkeeping' - a labour of love, by goalkeepers for goalkeepers and all who love, appreciate or want to learn about our wonderful craft, no matter what the sport.

'The One In A Team' by Sebastian Lasic

2

The role and importance of a goalkeeper

"Goalkeepers are, by definition, weirdos and odd ones out: they put their faces where others put their studs, and their chosen function in a sport defined by its flow and energy is one of apparent inaction followed by occasional moments of joy-killing intervention."

Simon Armitage, 'Why I Love Goalkeepers'[3]

This is not a history book. There are wonderful books on the history of goalkeeping[4] around and I have drawn inspiration and material from some of them in writing this one. The reason this book starts with a historical note on our wonderful craft is to acknowledge the immensely rich history of goalkeeping across many sports and to pay respect to our goalkeeping brothers and sisters. You may have idolised some of them as a child, played with or against others, or perhaps helped some of them grow up yourself. Some of our kind have even violently died while in goals! The vast majority of them you and I have never seen or heard of. But what all of us have shared is the thrill of keeping the space between the sticks and the net behind us locked up, thinking 'come on, beat me if you can' to the attackers bearing down on us. Understanding ourselves now and looking into the future would be impoverished without looking back to see where we came from and whose shoulders we stand on now. These are not just the shoulders of the adored giants but of all those thousands of goalkeepers in many sports at all levels. We have all stood in the goalmouth and faced the field in front of us, like some sort of renegade within the team[5]. This has made not just the position but the identity of a goalkeeper one the most revered, hated, feared and wanted one in any sport.

Where does goalkeeping come from? Good but a hard question to answer definitely. Versions of a dedicated 'guardian' of a particular end or scoring area may have existed in ancient sports. Some of these sports played on different continents are mentioned in reference books as the predecessors of modern games like football. As Jonathan Wilson writes in his wonderful book *The Outsider: A History of the Goalkeeper*[6], in the ancient Greek and Roman games of *phaininda* and *harpastum*[7] there had been a positioning of slower players around the back of the field in what Galen called *locus stantium*, loosely translated as standing or waiting room. These early games were largely serious and brutal affairs and, like many of the mob-like games, regulated by very few if any rules. In the case of Incas, losses in games like this were punishable by death. Imagine being the guardian who let that one through!

If we go by the criteria of the 'oldest sport with a goalkeeper played today', this would have to be hurling. Hurling is an ancient Irish game, still passionately played in Ireland, and dates back 3000 years. Similarly, lacrosse, played by the Native Americans for centuries, now does contain a position of goalkeeper, first formally mentioned in 1895.

For all the wonderfully rich and colourful histories of our craft in different sports, the one sport that stood out in terms of the age of records and the sheer volume of information on historical development of goalkeeping useful in writing this book is football (called soccer in some parts of the world). Football, and particularly its first codified rules in 1857, was also the precursor to many of the sports we know now, and therefore loosely forms the trunk of the 'family tree' of the sports looked at in this book.

Each of the sports with a goalkeeper has its own colourful history of the great cage men and women. In some sports, there are figures that stand out like synonyms for goalkeeping. In others, picking even the five 'best ever' is a book on its own. Beating them was or perhaps still is the ultimate challenge for the opposition players, scoring against them a mark of achievement and with it a mark of respect these goalkeepers command. The crowds usually come to see goals and 'results' but in the case of these goalkeeping legends - they came to see the opposite! The way they moved, saved, commanded, innovated, persisted, inspired ... But these immortals on the world stage are not the only goalkeepers revered and respected. At every level, there have been goalkeepers that remain to be talked about with reverence within that community. You don't have to be Yashin[8] to be admired for generations.

What has made these figures stand out? Reasons vary of course but innovation, longevity, extraordinary ability and notoriety are the common denominators across sports. All the innovative changes, particularly in the style and technique of goalkeeping, have come from someone thinking 'what if', having success with it and others copying, tweaking and developing it further. This process continues today. Some goalkeepers are known for their incredible longevity in goals. The combination of lower physical demands and longer maturation compared to the field players makes it easier to develop stability and consistency. These qualities are not to be messed with in a goalkeeper for as long as possible. Some goalkeepers are known for their incredible athleticism and a string of 'how did they possibly get that' moments that inspire their team and deflate the opposition. Others again are known for their flamboyance that sometimes has a darker, notorious side of 'crazy' goalkeepers. And some are just a complete package.

Many books, articles, even films have been made on the specialness of the role of a goalkeeper. Some of the greatest writers like Nabokov[9], a very keen goalkeeper himself during and after his studies at Cambridge, wrote of a goalkeeper as "the lone eagle, the man of mystery, the last defender… showing the gallant art of goalkeeping and the eccentricity of the role essentially ill-suited to English mentality."

At first, the goalkeeping role is a really weird one, as pointed out by this chapter's opening quote. On the face of it, we are anti-sport. We exist to deny goals that people come to see. Our best game, statistically at least, is the one we don't have to do much at all and our worst, statistically most likely again, when we are exhausted from physical activity. We would rather prevent a shot than save it, stop a goal than score it (OK, scoring one *is* a special thrill). We love getting in the way of and feel the impact of an object that can and does hurt, sometimes badly so. The only time the scoreboard moves is when we fail, not succeed. In most sports, the game play does not pause for celebrations when we do well, only when we fail. Our mistakes are the most obvious to even the most untrained eyes and most costly of any other role in the field. Add to that the different colours we stick out in and in some cases the extra gear we lug around and you really have something that is ... incredibly appealing!

Seen simplistically, the role of a goalkeeper is primarily one of a denier. The cleaner, the last defence, the insurance to save the team when the field players have failed. This may be the case sometimes and it makes the highlights reel of great saves. Overall though this is a pretty lazy and negative view of goal-keeping and indeed defence. In it, the goalkeeper merely waits to cover for the field players' mistakes. In turn, the field players may either slack off relying on a good goalkeeper to get them out of trouble or work overtime should the supposed denier behind them look like Swiss cheese. Neither of these creates trust!

Another way is seeing the goalkeeper as the builder of the foundation that any serious team serious about their chances cannot go without. Someone doing the ordinary but important jobs extraordinarily well, actively forcing a style of play the opposition may not like, closing space, distributing, proactively working together in sync with players to channel the ball to be easily stolen, saved or blocked, and reassuring their team with consistency. In this view, the question is not "what trouble can this goalkeeper get us out of?" but a lot more positively framed "what does having this goalkeeper afford us to do, build in the game, tournament or season?"

Similarly, when asked what is the job of a goalkeeper, the most immediate and common response is to 'stop shots going into the back of the net'. Well yes, but...

A few years ago I heard a story of an elite level coach, not a goalkeeper himself, responding to their goalkeeper's request for feedback on their game with three words only - "stop more shots". That was it! This may be fine for the little Under 9s but at the elite level, or in fact anything above the most beginning level, this is the *start*, not the end of conversation. The most rudimentary function of stopping shots of course must not be forgotten, but apart from it a goalkeeper has so many other important roles, especially as sports develop in speed, sophistication and rules.

Many of the games preceding today's versions allowed any players to defend their goal. For example, in the earliest versions of codified football anyone could take a 'fair catch' but not hold on to the ball. Once the role of a goalkeeper as a specialist stopper was born, the goalkeepers were often in direct physical threat of violence. Who wouldn't go and tackle that single guy with the ball so close to scoring a precious goal?

In water polo, the opposite was the case. With the first goals on the shore not in the water, the goalkeepers were allowed to charge and jump on the heads of the approaching attackers from dry land! The violence and no doubt injuries associated with goalkeeping must have hardly been a big attraction to the role. To prevent or at least minimise these excesses, the rule makers created exclusive zones and special use rules for goalkeepers. With these developments, the goalkeeper was not only more protected but their influence expanded. They became the first attacker as they were able to distribute the ball up the field more freely.

As the violence of the first versions of the games got curbed by the rules of contact further up the field, intelligent positioning of players in space became more and more important to teams. Who better to call the shots than the person closest to the action, most rested and with the best, widest and unimpeded view? In doing this, goalkeepers had to start communicating and coordinating their intentions with their players. And just like teams had realised their attack often starts from their goalkeeper, they increasingly realised their defence starts with the way they lose the ball. In some sports, this meant the goalkeeper as the defensive 'general' had a say in those ways too. Rule changes in some sports expanded goalkeepers' role even further and they could either be quickly substituted for an extra field player or advance up the field to be the loose extra player to pass or score.

The expansion of goalkeeper's role from the lone, brutalised stopper to something that resembles a conductor does not illustrate just the variety and complexity of the goalkeeper's role but also the ways and reasons for its growth over time. This brief timeline hopefully puts things in perspective and shows that 'stopping shots' that the mentioned coach wanted is just one, albeit important of course, aspect of the goalkeepers' job today.

So just how important is the role of a goalkeeper? Let's put this another way. I am not suggesting anyone should, but if you were a gambling cheat trying to fix a game, which of the players in a team would you go to first? Over time, goalkeepers have evolved to someone who holds the keys to the team's success. This of course has its pros and cons, discussed throughout the book. The words of my first coach who granted my wish to start specialist goalkeeper training remain ringing in my ears all these decades on: "There is nothing like being a great goalkeeper and nothing like being a bad one." Throughout my career and while researching for this book, I have never heard the answer to the question "How much is the goalkeeper worth to a team?" with something that indicates unimportance or perhaps even parity with another role on the field. A hockey coach I interviewed for this book described the goalkeeper as "the thumb of the hand", others used "the house foundation" and similar analogies. When asked to express the 'worth' of a goalkeeper to a team in percentages, I have never heard of anything below 50%. The question here is not about calculating an accurate percentage of course but to illustrate the point of importance of a goalkeeper to the team.

Speaking of percentages, a simple percentage of shots faced and saved can easily be calculated and good goalkeepers definitely have higher numbers there. As shown in the table[10] below, the save ratios vary across different sports, all with their nature of the game and rules. What is not shown in the table but consistently observed across sports though is the correlation between the best teams and their goalkeeper's high save percentages. In other words, good teams have good goalkeepers, and a great team with a poor or average goalkeeper would be a strange anomaly. Of course it is hard to untangle and specify exactly how strong this correlation with team success is caused by the efforts of the goalkeeper alone and how much or their teammates. Such an effort would actually miss the point of modern goalkeeping as a role that is not separate from but highly integrated within the team.

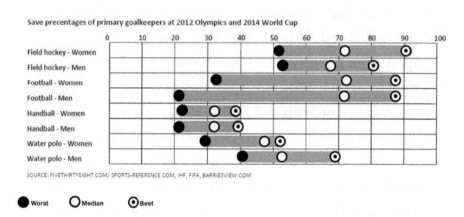

Save precentages of primary goalkeepers at 2012 Olympics and 2014 World Cup

SOURCE: FIVETHIRTYEIGHT.COM/ SPORTS-REFERENCE.COM, IHF, FIFA, BARRIESVIEW.COM

● Worst ○ Median ◉ Best

Source: https://fivethirtyeight.com/features/which-olympic-sport-is-hardest-on-its-goalies/

In his publication[11], a fellow water polo goalkeeper (and a legend at that) Craig Wilson puts it like this:

A goalie's impact on the game can be easily expressed with simple arithmetic. In an average water polo game there are usually 20 or so shots taken on goal. An average goalie will block 40% and a strong

goalie will block 60% of the shots. With the numbers as a benchmark, a strong goalie performance will create a 4-5 goal difference per game. Show me a player that regularly scores 4 to 5 goals a game.

Important? No, crucial.

So what does a modern goalkeeper look like? Answering this question might have to start with a broader one: "What does the modern game look like?" While again sports differ in their development, there seems to be a common thread. In their desire to be more spectacular and attract larger audiences, sports games are becoming faster, more mobile and generate more shots on goal. This has not just been a marketing exercise but a combination of development in physical abilities of players and rule changes that discourage heavy physical contact and static defending. What does this mean for goalkeepers?

Apart from the bread and butter shot-stopping, goalkeepers' positioning, anticipation, distribution into attack and coordination of movement with defenders are becoming more important than ever. Due to the greater speed and mobility, managing the corridors through which the ball and opposition can travel by careful blocking and positioning of oneself and defenders is an increasingly important skill of a modern goalkeeper. Add to this the increasing demand to develop and master ball handling and shooting to the levels no different to the field players and we can see how the goalkeeper is quickly turning from a one-job specialist to a multi-skilled athlete[12]. It would be reasonable to predict that these trends are likely to continue. The intensity, speed, stakes and with them the expectations of what goalkeepers can and ought to do will continue to rise across different sports. With reaction speeds approaching human limits, as discussed in chapter 4, the rationalisation of movement, coordination with players and perhaps developments in mental and not just physical capabilities may be the new edge in goal-keeping in the years ahead.

How much of this development will fundamentally change the position of a goalkeeper? A reasonable question that no doubt many will try to find answers to. But let's consider the second part of that question - the *position* of a goalkeeper.

We don't just 'play in goals' - we *are* goalkeepers. 'Goalkeeper' is a playing position, *being* a goalkeeper is a part of our identity. For some among us, it is one of the most defining parts of who we are. One way to imagine our identity is to see it as a coherent, ongoing story about ourselves that we create and make sense of. The more we tell and perform the story *of* and *about* ourselves, the more we *become* the story. In our case, the more important 'being a goalkeeper' is to us the more it will affect our life at different stages. Because of the uniqueness of our playing position and its responsibilities, identifying as a goalkeeper may be and often is very strong. We can't help standing out in a team, even when full of people with specialist roles within it. This affects, sometimes very deeply, the way we think, feel and act not just as a goalkeeper but as a person on the whole. By becoming a goalkeeper, we also become a part of the story of goalkeepers, the stuff of this book. We simultaneously contrib-ute *to* it while being shaped *by* it and its history, practices and changing expectations of what being a goalkeeper involves.

Why labour this point? Go and observe people, particularly children, and note what happens when they begin to *identify* as goalkeepers, not just as someone playing in goals. Watch how the level of care they take rises right in front of your eyes! What about the phrase 'once a goalkeeper - always a goalkeeper' we hear sometimes? We may not have played at their level but we can relate to other goalkeepers, work with them, understand them better once we have identified as a fellow goalkeeper, not just stood in the goalmouth a couple of times out of either sheer curiosity or necessity when no one else would.

Importantly though, our identity is *not* a static product but a dynamic process, a constant interaction between ourselves and our environment. The more important our identity as a goalkeeper is to us the more we want to have it nurtured by the environment in which we operate. If there is a mismatch between what we bring to the environment (team, club, coaches...) and what the environment expects of us and affords us, we suffer not just as a 'playing position' but as a person.

For example, not having a goalkeeper coach or avoiding any work with goalkeepers may send a message of "I don't really care" not just about goalkeeping but about the goalkeeper as a person. The goalkeeper can't do it all alone. On the other side, a good environment doesn't automatically make the goalkeeper either. Great coaches and training facilities surely help but they are no guarantee that a goalkeeper will fully develop their potential in goals. They need to *want* to identify and be identified as a goalkeeper and *want* to have a good story to tell to themselves and others as one.

Consider this next time you hear about (un)happy goalkeepers and reasons for it. Nobody wants the story of themselves as a goalkeeper to be a sad one.

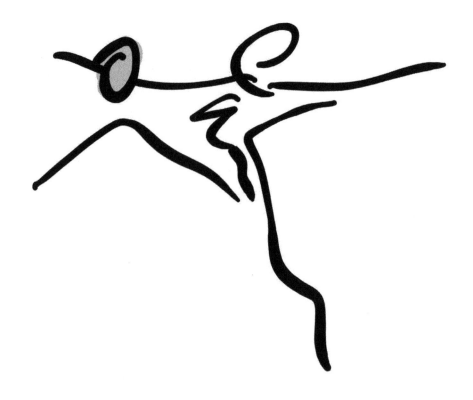

'Like A Cat' by Sebastian Lasic

3

Moving like a cat

"And that was the first moment I understood how deeply the Keeper's teaching had reached into me. I did not remember the jaguar. I did not have time to remember, or think about, the big cat. It was not a matter of imitating her beautiful agility, the way she shifted herself in the middle of her leap. At that moment I was her. Like hers, my body knew what to do. So instead of simply falling to the ground once I had made the save, I twisted so that my hips and legs pulled my body past the post..."

'El Gato' (The Cat) in 'Keeper'[13]

You may not be a 'cat' person and like cats. You may be even allergic to them. However, I do presume you have seen them move and jump. One of nature's smoothest and most efficient hunters and killers. Their balance, poise, positioning and their agile leap like an uncoiled spring towards the target are something to be if not studied at least admired by goalkeepers as, in so many ways, human imitators of these creatures.

Angles, positioning and movement. The stuff of this chapter is so essential, automated and internalised by an experienced goalkeeper in any sport that it feels like breathing. But even the greatest expert was once a novice and they had to learn where and how to move across the goalmouth. There is a good chance that the most goalkeepers' first lesson and advice were about where to stand in goals. When any goalkeeper, let alone an expert one, fails to follow the basic principles described below it looks like, feels like and often results in, costly failure.

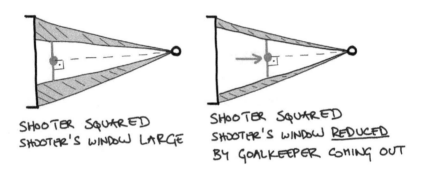

SHOOTER SQUARED
SHOOTER'S WINDOW LARGE

SHOOTER SQUARED
SHOOTER'S WINDOW REDUCED
BY GOALKEEPER COMING OUT

Every sport with a manual on goalkeeping will have two dimensional images similar to the ones above. They imagine the goalkeeper's reach like an impenetrable wall facing the shooter, travelling on an arc from side to side facing shots from different angles. Excuse the math-speak here but in its universal geometrical sense, the goalkeeper ideally describes an isosceles triangle with the ball as the vertex and the symmetry line running from the middle of the goalkeeper's chest that sits 90 degrees or 'square' to the shooter. This optimises two important objectives. Firstly, it leaves the least amount of 'shooter's window', the space out of reach of the goalkeeper that a shooter can squeeze the ball through to score. Secondly, it prioritises the coverage of the near post (some sports use terms like 'short corner, 'near corner', 'close corner'), often the safest, nearest, largest and most tempting shooting choice. Even the youngest of goalkeepers quickly understand these basic principles but even the most experienced goalkeepers sometimes fail to observe them! This means they can never be practised enough.

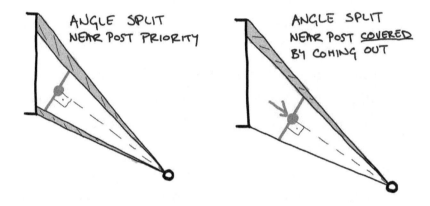

Mastering the arc of travel across the goalmouth is essential. However, the symmetry line we get from squaring and 'splitting' the shooter provides another advantage. It is a perfect path to travel forward to further close the shooter's window. Sports differ in the ease of fast movement forward and the benefits of doing so. The faster the goalkeeper is able to move forward and the greater the benefit of doing so, the more expectation there is on the goalkeeper to learn this skill. Futsal and handball goalkeepers will use this a lot more than for example water polo goalkeepers and their training reflects that. However, the principle of travelling forward is geometrically sound and applicable to all sports.

Moving forward or 'off the line' not only reduces or even closes the shooters window and increases chances of a save. It also adds two further possibilities - block or steal. In this book, a *save* is a successful reaction to a shot that a goalkeeper has reasonable time to react to. A *block* is a premeditated move forward into a position where the goalkeeper will most likely be hit by the ball. When blocking, the goalkeeper has no time to react to it but has mostly or completely closed the shooters' window in three-dimensional space. The ball has nowhere else to go but into the goalkeeper's body or wide of goals. All sports have this distinction but due to their proximity to shooters and ball speed, handball, futsal, ice hockey and even water polo are particularly good sports to see the difference between a save and a block and learn from.

Venturing further and sometimes quite far off their (goal) line, a goalkeeper can turn into a field player to *steal* or 'sweep' the ball and prevent the shot from being taken at all. Skills equivalent to those of a field player are essential here. A clumsy goalkeeper is an easy target for hungry strikers and sometimes unconsciously biased referees who don't let get goalkeepers off lightly doing a field players' job.

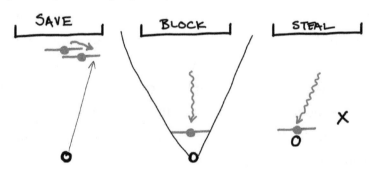

The covering of angles and moving off the line comes with a few important warnings, pictured below.

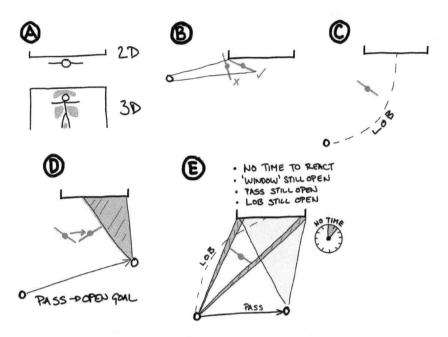

Goalkeeper's reach is assumed as a 'wall' when represented on a two-dimensional screen or paper but doesn't show the difficulties in the third dimension **(A)**. Some of the spots near or above the body in some sports are the hardest to get to! Getting angry with the goalkeeper for letting through a shot around the body that on paper looked theirs may sometimes be an unfairly harsh thing to do.

Coming out and off the line involves the trade off between reducing the shooter's window, blocking and stealing one the one side, and possible dangers on the other. One of these dangers is over-covering the corner **(B)**. Extending arms well beyond the posts is a waste and may indeed risk a corner in some sports.

As shot angles become very acute, some sports actually encourage goalkeepers to step back to the line and not square the shooter perfectly, as long as the near corner is safely covered. This improves the vision of the whole field and makes any movement to cover or prevent further shots much easier.

Another danger in coming out of the goals or 'off line' inappropriately is the opening of the airspace above for a chip or lob over the goalkeeper's head **(C)**. This of course applies to some sports more than others. I haven't seen too many goals from lobs in hockey of any type, have you?

The next danger is opening the 'passing lane' to another player that makes a later intervention an impossible one and ends up in an open goal as the angle and space to get across to cover any part of the goal is simply too large for the goalkeeper to cover quickly **(D)**.

The last of the dangers of coming off the line poorly is being stuck in 'no man's land'. This is a combination of the previous three dangers. The narrowing of the shooter's window doesn't leave enough time to react and make a save, there is still too much space for an effective block, the airspace above may be open and a pass to another player is a certain goal **(E)**. Danger, danger!

The essential question in teaching, using and analysing movement in goalkeeping is "What is the fastest way to get to the desired point to act from with a minimum of effort?" The introduction to this chapter uses a lyrical description of goalkeepers like cats as smooth movers, pouncing effectively. But cats are also seemingly very lazy creatures. I'm not sure if they actually do but they certainly look like they often ask the question "What movement is necessary?" And it is a good question!

In terms of geometry and expense of energy, the shortest, straightest possible line is best. But that's just one part of the story. Two-dimensional diagrams may show the shortest path to travel but they don't show the best ways of getting there and acting effectively from it. When the goalkeeper gets to the wanted point, we would also want them to get in the 'poise' to act from as quickly as possible. In this book, I use the term *poise* (also called 'basic position', 'stance', 'stand' or 'set' in different sports) to describe the *basic position from which a goalkeeper initiates the movement towards the ball*.

The poise may change slightly, depending on the distance from the shooter. It tends to be more upright for fast reaction to shots around the body or with a more pronounced forward lean to generate an extension boost from the trunk and legs to reach shots laterally or high above. In most sports, the position is one of balance with the *centre of gravity* (COG)[14] slightly ahead of the hips with mostly the legs and the trunk providing the required stability.

In rudimentary physics terms, COG is an imaginary equilibrium point, a three-dimensional fulcrum around which the weight of the body is equally supported. If you imagine balancing a goalkeeper on a pin, COG is the very tip of that pin. From this point, the goalkeeper can rotate and travel most freely in *any direction*. The key phrase here is *any direction* because that is exactly what we want our goalkeeper to be able to do - go in any direction with the greatest ease. When standing straight, our COG lies within our body. The moment we start to lean in any direction and especially if severely so, COG moves and may end up outside our body. That's fine, provided we have the support.

RESTORING THE CENTRE OF GRAVITY

When moved suddenly, the aim is to restore or set the COG in the desired position as quickly as possible. The larger and more singular (for example a lunge) the move to the desired spot, the greater the inertia and the harder and more time consuming it is to restore the COG to 'poise'. Such big movements also make a deflection, a bane of existence to goalkeepers in any sport, very difficult or even impossible to handle. If moving or landing heavily, second or third effort saves are equally difficult if not impossible. And when 'wrong footed' by a shot, you truly understand where the COG is and where you would like it instead. This leads to a conclusion that small and fast corrections of our support to reach this equilibrium we can act from are much more efficient than large, heavy moves. Seen this way, it is easy to understand why the ground-based goalkeepers prize the shuffle of light, fast and nimble feet over heavy stomps and water polo goalkeepers smooth surface glides and steps rather than big sinking lunges around the place.

The 'poise' position is similar across sports, with COG slightly ahead the hips and legs (mostly) providing the base of support. Tipping forward a little more is sometimes necessary to give the goalkeeper a momentum boost that comes from contracting and expanding their trunk. Such a boost may be necessary to reach further but is costly in terms of 'save time' (the time a goalkeeper has to save the shot, more on that in the next chapter). Speaking of tipping and leaning, the ground-based goalkeepers will tell you that sitting back on your heels and having your COG behind you is particularly dangerous as it makes your feet 'heavy' and 'rooted to the spot'. This is because you need the large muscle groups of legs and your core to move your feet rather than the more responsive smaller muscles in the balls of your feet. In the water, 'sitting back' severely reduces your ability to jump and tends to open the shooter's window as you are more likely to jump backwards. And if you have ever skated on ice, you probably know what happens if you lean backwards. No matter how skilled or strong you are, gravity does not care.

It is an axiom across sports that the bigger the surface area (body and/or equipment) we can put behind the ball the better our chances of saving, blocking or stealing that shot. While the described nimble and balanced movements are the preferred option to achieve this, some tipping, dropping, jumping and lunging wildly may sometimes be necessary, especially in desperate situations.

Sometimes, you just need to lean back to get a few more precious milliseconds or millimetres to reach that shot. Sometimes, getting in the way of the ball with balance-ignoring, gravity-defying reckless abandon will produce some memorable saves and adrenaline rushes but counting on it every time is unrealistic. The best goalkeepers can be extraordinary when extraordinary is required, but for most of the time, they just do the ordinary things extraordinarily well.

Exercising spatial awareness and orientation can never be practised enough from very early on. The essential first step, and the easiest, is for goalkeepers to understand their own orientation in goal, then squaring the shooter and angles on or close to the goal line. Next is movement along and off the imaginary arc. This may be conceptually easy to show on paper but can be difficult to master and therefore takes longer time to fully develop. There are two key reasons for it.

Firstly, efficient ways of moving across and out of goals are not necessarily innate. They must be learned and practised, keeping in mind the goalkeeper's stage of physical development and knowledge of the game. Secondly, coming 'off the (goal) line' in particular requires a degree of judgement that only deliberate practice and experience can develop. Goalkeepers become great judges not just of appropriate distances to cover but their ability to cover them and ways of acting from various points. These aspects change, sometimes dramatically so, as the goalkeepers' knowledge of themselves and the game changes with their level of physical and psychological maturity. Patience and a sense of bigger picture are absolutely essential.

One of the many things goalkeepers can simply never practice enough is their agility. *Agility* is understood here as the controlled ability of goalkeepers to move and change direction and position of their body and their COG quickly and effectively. Agility [15]is a combination of reflexes, coordination, balance, speed, and (appropriate) response to the changing situation. Goalkeepers can benefit from performing any activity where they would constantly check if "the distance [from the ball] and body position right now gives them the best chance of success" and dynamically adjust to it. From warm ups and general agility to sport-specific exercises, the more agile goalkeeper the better the chances of success.

But while an agile, cat-like goalkeeper may look a better prospect than someone with stiffer, 'wooden' moves, they are not guaranteed success. The ability to move into certain positions quickly and efficiently is one thing. Understanding when to do so and what to do with it is another. This 'goalkeeper intelligence' and ability to read the game lies at the heart of the next chapter.

This chapter started with a quote about cat-like movement from 'Keeper', the award winning book by the sadly late Mal Peet. If you ever want to give a present to a young goalkeeper, or one young at heart, I recommend getting a copy of it. A beautiful piece of youth literature where the story is fictional, parallels with life lyrical, but there is much truth and beauty about goal-keeping in it.

'Gotcha!' by Sebastian Lasic

4

Reading the game

"In the beginner's mind there are many possibilities, in the expert's mind there are few."

Shunryu Suzuki

Knowing where and how to move is of little use to a goal-keeper if they are unable to move to the right spot at the right time. To get there, goalkeepers need to be able not just to physically see but effectively read the play unfolding in front of them. Arguably they need to read the play even more and better than the field players. The two main reasons for this are simple - goalkeepers' mistakes are very expensive and the times to spot and react very, very short. This is where goalkeepers need to use their powers of focus and anticipation. And the good news about these powers? While they may look like it at times, they are not some magically given superpowers. They *can* be trained and improved.

Let's start with a few questions from the basic science of seeing and reaction. Here we go...

What is the size of the focus area where we, humans, see things in high definition? Answer: around 20 millimetres. That's the size of a very small coin! To see our surroundings clearly, our focus shifts constantly in small jumps called saccades (you are doing it right now reading this) or in steady movements called smooth pursuits (put a finger in front of you and track the tip of it). This scattering of focus is very helpful in processing lots of information, with the mind filling the blanks and making sense of it all.

How long does it take to blink? Answer: between 300 and 400 milliseconds (ms), roughly a third of a second[16] (one millisecond is one thousandth of a second). How about a basic, common to all healthy people, un-trainable, reaction to a single, simple visual stimulus like a small flashing light, in perfect lab conditions? Around 200ms, roughly a fifth of a second. When given a choice to pick between two correct responses, the reaction time goes up to about 400ms and increases with the number and complexity of choices on offer, according to the scientifically very robust Hick's Law[17]. When under severe physical load or with the age past our physical prime, the numbers rise again.[18]

Let us now look at average *save times* to the most common shots in different sports. Here the term *save time* (expressed in milliseconds or thousands of a second) refers to the time it takes the ball to travel from the release point of the shot to the goal line. If the goalkeeper is off the line and even closer to the shooter, the save time is even shorter. Now keep in mind that during this time, the goalkeeper has to:

- spot the stimulus (ball or puck travelling towards them)
- choose the appropriate response (left? right? above? two hands? stick? ...)
- perform the movement to intercept the shot (in some sports this may mean moving, usually laterally, for several metres!)

Sport	Shot speed (in km/h)			Distance	
	Max Rec'd	Fast (80%)	Avg (60%)	Common	Long
Football	154	123	92	7	15
Ice hockey	175	140	105	4	9
Handball	139	111	83	5	8
Water Polo	102	82	61	5	8
Field hockey	145	116	87	7	15
Hurling	180	144	108	7	15
Lacrosse	193	154	116	7	15

Sport	Save time (Common distance)			Save time (Long distance)		
	Max	Fast (80%)	Avg (60%)	Max	Fast (-15%)	Avg(-35%)
Football	164	205	273	351	438	584
Ice hockey	82	103	137	185	231	309
Handball	129	162	216	207	259	345
Water Polo	176	221	294	282	353	471
Field hockey	174	217	290	372	466	621
Hurling	140	175	233	300	375	500
Lacrosse	131	163	218	280	350	466

= less time than a standard human reaction to a visual stimulus (200ms)

= less time than an average human blink of an eye (350 milliseconds)

This table is for illustration purposes only, see Notes for details.[19]

Anything strikes you here, given that the average human blink lasts about 350 milliseconds? Yes, for the majority of the shots they face, goalkeepers across different sports have less time than it takes to blink to react, choose and move. Not much time is it? And while the basic human reaction time has stayed the same for arguably millions of years, further developments in the biomechanics of shooting, strength of shooters and sports equipment to produce faster shot speeds are well underway and are likely to continue. For example, several handball coaches and goalkeepers mentioned the recent developments in creating a ball that requires no resin that players traditionally use to improve their grip. The new ball will improve ball handling and with it increase the speed and versatility of shots. Similarly, the proliferation of lighter and stronger carbon fibre sticks with a precisely customised amount of 'flex' and centre of gravity in hockey is not going to make shooting slower or less accurate either. And more...

You would be excused to think the goalkeepers' lives are just going to get even tougher. Just how do goalkeepers then manage to see, let alone make comfortable saves of these shots even now? Looks like magic! Let's look at the first of the two connected powers that help goalkeepers weave this magic - focus.

"Watch the ball!" This would have to be one of the most common and frequent shouts to goalkeepers from the side of the playing field. It is also something thousands of goalkeepers have whispered to themselves in the goalmouth. I could not find an empirical study, just plenty of personal experience as a goalkeeper and a coach to confirm this. You probably don't need (m) any empirical studies to confirm that watching a projectile flying towards you is a good idea and that it is easier to stop it if you are looking at it. What the research has shown however is that there are better ways of doing so.

Expert goalkeepers constantly scan their environment and take in visual, aural and tactile clues from which they read what is happening now and what is about to happen in the game. The more this process is automated through repetition, the more it becomes unconscious and the more it shortens the processing time. Keep this reasonable and scientifically validated line of thought in your mind as we will expand on it later here and elsewhere in the book. For now, let's look just at the vision. Intuitively, we would think that the more goalkeepers scan for and spot the clues the better. All good so far. And the quicker their eyes scan the more clues they will pick up and the more successful they will be in performing the required motor action, right?

This was the hypothesis posited by Joan Vickers, a pioneer in the field of visual perception and cognition. She was interested in what the elite athletes as the experts watch just before they execute a critical motor skill compared to novices. What she found in her research in athletes from various sports surprised her and certainly did not confirm her initial hypothesis. Instead of scattering their vision to pick up more clues, the experts intently focused on the target object just before, in the case of goalkeepers, it began to travel towards them. Their gaze seemingly calmed down and 'locked on' the target about to be flung towards them just before the final critical movements. They did so earlier, then maintained their focus on it for longer than novices.

Vickers named this time of slowing down the constant and jumpy saccadic movement *quiet eye* (QE)[20]. In the case of ice hockey goalkeepers, earlier onset of QE in the early stages of the shot, gave the expert goalkeepers enough critical information about the trajectory (speed and direction) of the puck. This was especially effective when corroborated with other clues (for example, stance of the shooter, aural clues and more). The experts goalkeepers not only 'locked on' earlier but also tracked the object longer than the novices, giving them more accurate calculations of the trajectory of the shot and ultimately the contact with the puck.[21]

This is all fine but you probably think "hey, my sport is too dynamic to just stare at the ball all day." Yes, you are absolutely right! The focus shifts and drifts among different things during the game but the difference between experts and novices is that the former know not just how but when and what to focus on to maximise their chances of a successful intervention. They scan for clues all the time but zero in on the ball just before it is released and follow it along the way. Hopefully next time you hear a coach yelling to the goalkeeper to "watch the ball", you understand *when* the goalkeeper should be doing it and *why* the coach is saying it. This is of course an axiom only for shots when there is time for the goalkeeper to meaningfully track the ball to perform a save. If performing a close range block with no time to meaningfully react to the direction of the shot, the goalkeeper's eyes may *not* fully turn away from the ball or even shut but instead rest on another clue-generating spot (for example, shooter's eyes, stance or something else).

Goalkeepers and their coaches have long used various methods to improve visual focus. I am not influenced by any of the particular methods to promote here and I will leave you to judge what may be a good fit for you in your context. However, Vickers' research showed that even the simplest things like writing a number on the bottom of the ball to recognise, simple occlusions (hiding/revealing), or eye tracking using small objects and/or smaller than-regular balls (eg tennis or golf balls) showed a notable improvement in early onset and longer duration of QE, and this supported better decision making[22]. In addition, and with perhaps larger budgets, many labs and sporting organisations have been experimenting with theories like Biological Motion Perception[23], using 3D projections and virtual reality to train focus and decision making. People are doing so not just because it is interesting (I for one would love to learn more!) but because it brings results in the areas of diminishing *save times* and with that the margins between success and failure.

OK, so visual focus gives goalkeepers a better idea of where the shot will go. But what about those reaction times again? Let's check out another important power that helps to read the game - anticipation.

In his seminal research on (in)voluntary reactions, Benjamin Libet[24] [25]asked the participants (all healthy adults) to flick their wrists whenever they chose to and not as a response to a stimulus. Consistently, their brain unconsciously fired 350-400ms *before they thought* they decided to move. Libet called the time between the subconscious firing and the conscious thought *readiness potential* (RP). At the end of RP and the first point of conscious thought, the participants' minds acted like a switch - they could approve the movement and proceed or veto the act and stop it altogether. The first actual movement of the wrist occurred 200ms later, roughly 550ms or a whole half a second after the first electrical signal in the brain. An eternity in goalkeeper land!

Apart from the philosophically interesting question 'who, or rather what, then begins the brain function' (do we have a free will?), Libet also posits that voluntary acts that become "somewhat automatic" can be performed with no reportable conscious wish or trigger to do so and with minimal RP. Let's add to this the findings of an MIT study[26] that humans can identify images with meaning in as little as 13ms, a fraction of the 300ms it takes to blink an eye. What do we get? We get a mind subconsciously triggering, then consciously making meaning, deciding and initiating or vetoing a 'somewhat automated' act not within half a second but a mere few milliseconds. There is hope for goalkeepers after all it seems.

Imagine driving a car. The first few times behind the wheel, you focus totally on the basics of gas, break, gears, turns and rules. Chances are you respond to emerging situations with big halts and wheel corrections. After several hours of driving, your driving becomes smoother and you pass the test to go on the road. You predict the most obvious situations (wet road, heavy traffic) and act to negotiate them safely. Now let us imagine you drive a certain route every day and you soon begin to expect a certain pattern of events to happen at certain points of the drive. After weeks, months of driving that same route, you know almost exactly what will happen at different points at different times of the day or season and you simply look for the smallest clues to confirm it. Driving that route becomes so automatic you sometimes barely realise, even forget in your 'expert amnesia' that you're driving. In this state, you free your working memory to do something else (hopefully not checking your phone...) but you are still able to react and quickly correct course if needed. You have gone from consciously incompetent when you first sat behind the wheel to consciously competent to unconsciously competent driving that route and others (this 'competency model' is outlined further in chapter 9).

Exactly the same thing happens in goalkeeping. When we start as goalkeepers, we have no idea where the ball will go and we simply react, usually with a relative delay, to the ball flying in our direction. Very soon, we recognise patterns and begin to predict where the ball or players will go. We have a thought about what will happen in order to maximise our chances of success. But that still sounds like a gamble. After a while and based on further experience that takes into account the context of the shot or move, we begin to expect the most likely outcomes. As we progress further, we begin to anticipate. At this, the final stage, we seemingly know what is going to happen and even the smallest signs of it are enough to confirm it.

We have gone from waiting for something to happen, to reacting to it happening, to predicting what will happen, to expecting it to happen, to finally knowing what is highly likely to happen and, importantly, knowing almost automatically and instinctively what to do when it does.

But isn't this anticipation still just a guess, and by extension, are the best goalkeepers just the best 'guessers' then? There is a massive difference between guessing and anticipation. Guessing is often the result of poor or no planning, it is random and requires no experience. Guessing is also a conscious process that, as just demonstrated, takes up many important milliseconds of time. As a result, guesses are a hit-and-miss chance. When unsuccessful, they usually look either 'jerky' and mis-timed, with goalkeepers acting too early with a premeditated move in the wrong direction, or too late, resulting in a panicked and inadequate move.

Anticipation on the other side is a result of established patterns in the goalkeeper's mind that will trigger or veto a conscious act at almost subconscious speeds to elicit the best response in a smooth, efficient and timely way. Sure, in a dynamic environment like sport, anticipation still contains an element of chance. However, this is a result of deliberate thought, planning, and practice over time, adjusted for what is going on at that very moment. This is the essence of Suzuki's 'few possibilities' of an expert mentioned in the opening quote of the chapter. This is also why "the seconds of the greats last longer than those of normal people" as Ajax manager David Endt put it. And goal-keepers certainly can and do develop that.

You may be familiar with the phrase 'muscle memory'. It's a catchy way of putting it but it's technically incorrect[27], a misnomer. Sure, muscles do gain and retain the strength to act in certain ways and patterns. This strength and ability also dissipates, at different rates, during the periods of inaction. This is the old 'use it or lose it' principle. However, muscles themselves do not 'hold a memory' of what to do. That is stored elsewhere.

The places that make the super smooth, unconscious-like automation described above possible are the basal ganglia and the cerebellum. These are the small areas of the brain lying under the cortex, the big, 'thinking', upper part of the brain. Basal ganglia initiate and cerebellum (size of an egg but containing about half of all our neurons!) controls and corrects ongoing movements. Memories created in these 'lower brain'[28] areas render our movements almost like the unconscious reflexes while freeing the working memory to scan and consider other tasks, much like a writer who focuses on the content rather than the mechanics of handwriting. Next time you practice, just know that every jump, stretch, dive, glide, block and other goalkeeping action can add and/or deepen a notch in the cerebellum[29].

I never liked the phrase "practice makes perfect." I prefer the great Bobby Robson's version: "Practice makes permanent!" The quality and not just the quantity of practice matters. We increasingly know why Robson's rework of an old truism is right and this field of science is rapidly making new discoveries that goalkeepers would benefit from. I don't know about you but I certainly want to explore more in this area.

Speaking of practice, what are the implications of this 'imprinting' on our inner parts of the brain for training and improving anticipation? Is lots of repetition all we need to do and worry about? Yes and no. Yes, we need experience, the quantity of time and exposure, but that does not guarantee expertise, the (high) standard of what we do.

The words *experience* and *expertise* are sometimes used as synonyms, substitutes for each other. Of course the more experienced goalkeepers tend to be greater experts at goalkeeping but experience and expertise are not the same thing. Both terms are value judgements *in the context* they are used. For example, a talented 13 year old goalkeeper and a veteran who has been facing amateur Sunday League shots for twenty years may both be far from World League standards but they are both considered 'expert' in their contexts.

Similarly, the 13 year-old who has been playing for two years is 'experienced' compared to their peer who started last week, but still a pup compared to a 'less experienced' goalkeeper in the Sunday League with only six compared to twenty years of goalkeeping like our veteran mentioned before.

Why bother pointing out this distinction between expertise and experience? Mostly because it is important to recognise the appropriate level of expertise (standard) in 'pitching' goalkeeper training and expectations. Appropriately set expectations based on the level of observed *expertise* are necessary to push the goalies outside their comfort zone without 'killing' them with things they are not ready for and/or capable despite their *experience*. This also avoids, or at least reduces, the amount of hair pulling and lament by coaches along the lines of 'a 14 year old goalkeeper should be able to do that.'

Yes, it is great and absolutely necessary to have standards and expectations but recognising and putting the energy into working with what the goalkeeper in front of you *has* is arguably a lot more productive than complaining about what they *don't have* but perhaps should at a particular age or level.

This is especially important when working with young goalkeepers. Pitching training and games at a (too) low level of expertise may result in experienced but incompetent goalkeepers. I have seen too many goalkeepers with many years of experience of playing who didn't do nor understand some of the fundamentals of the job. I couldn't entirely blame them either as nobody taught them while they probably never asked themselves. On the other hand, too many and/or unrealistic expectations of expertise (again, not to be confused with the relative experience) too early on and we may unnecessarily frustrate that promising youngster and ourselves. Expecting a child to do things exactly as that World Cup winner on TV may be well intended but counterproductive. It takes time.

One cannot be a master without being an apprentice. Spending time and effort in getting the basic mechanics of movement and understanding of the game right is well worth the patience and a few goals early on the way to mastery. Establishing patterns that are easy to remember and ingrain seems to be one of the key ways to achieve it. For example, Aljaž Pavlič, EHF Master Coach and an elite level handball goalkeeper himself, speaks of instilling the constant cycle of *set - focus - react* from the youngest goalkeepers to the Champions League standards. This 'in game' cycle is in many ways similar to the cycle of development that many others, including myself, have used across different sports. The words might differ slightly but the essential points of the continuous cycle are the same: *learn - prepare - act.*

In the *learn* phase we consciously process the what, when, who, why by recording, reflecting and evaluating. This is our big, slow brain at work. A lot of this work takes place before and after the action. 'Action' here could be as short as the next shot, or a training, a game, all the way to a tournament, league or season.

The essential question in this phase is "what can I/we learn from this?" Noticing and analysing patterns, variations and deviations is of course essential. However, beware of possible 'paralysis by analysis', especially where there is lots of increasingly easily generated data of all kinds (video, statistics). Such paralysis can be avoided by asking good, critical questions. Generating countless and possibly quite creative solutions but without really figuring out the problem is a recipe for frustration down the track. Asking "what really is the problem that this is a solution to?" can avoid a lot of it.

In the next, *prepare* stage, we start to narrow the options down, reading and anticipating the most likely ones to unfold and getting physically and mentally ready for the response 'right here, right now'. The biggest dangers here are fear and doubt. This is because they both force us to leave the moment, the right *now*, to think of the past or the future beyond the immediate setting. Anyone who has second-guessed, over-complicated or choked at crucial points during a game, even a season, is a testament to this danger. Be present in the present!

At the *act* stage there is no time to think and consider things. The cerebellum kicks in and we simply uncoil, without the conscious thoughts and fears that would slow us down or distract us. We commit, take the leap and fly!

Repeating such a cycled pattern until automation then frees the resources to fit the real-time information gathered by the senses with the information from the larger context (pre-set instructions, tactics, positions etc.) before and during a game, training, even a season. Given that they have the physical attributes and fitness to do so, goalkeepers who are superior processors of this information regularly intervene in the right place at the right time. They seemingly see and know a step or two ahead of the game. How frustrating for the opposition!

And just how much of this is all just innate, a matter of natural talent? While a natural ability to 'read the play' is definitely an asset, I always liked the quote "hard work beats talent when talent doesn't work hard enough." Oh yes, reading the play can definitely be worked on! The most obvious strategy is of course watching. There is much to learn and enjoy from watching lots of our sport and at *any* level too (and don't forget other sports and goalkeepers in them too!). Watching those above us in skill makes us want to be like them, watching those below us in skill validates our own progression. Watching those we currently play with and against gives us the competitive edge. Things like scouting, simulations, diaries, analysis, visualisation of individual shooters, teams and their patterns of shooting and play has been the smorgasbord of available options to improve focus, anticipation and decision making since the start of any sport. Technology has certainly improved the range of ways we can use to improve our reading of the game and there are many products and services available that combine training of visual perception with decision making.

Regardless of the method or product used to train anticipation and decision making, even a little of the above to improve beyond 'just playing' is better than nothing, as long as it is appropriate for the goalkeeper(s) in question. If you are a football goalkeeper, watching Ronaldo shooting in high tech 3D may be fun but is probably not going to do much for your own goalkeeping anticipation (unless of course you are playing at Champions League level and likely to face him). If you are serious about developing your own goalkeeping, it would be far more useful to watch, record, spot patterns, predict the next moves by your peers, even your likely opponents, in person or on screen. This is especially powerful you think of and visualise the probable patterns, clues and cues before and then see them during the game. This way, you read the play (and perhaps your opposition) like a book and the game feels like a movie based on that book. You know what is going to happen, you are just checking the script, ready to notice and handle deviations from it. This, combined with the thousands of repetitions of that jump, dive or block you can do without thinking about it, is the goalkeepers' 'superpower'.

Or as Bruce Lee said, "I fear not the man who has practised 10,000 kicks once, but I fear the man who has practised one kick 10,000 times."

'Move' by Sebastian Lasic

5

Fit and able

"Oh, that hurt. I am NOT a runner."

This was no famous person. It was me, about ten years ago after a pretty slow and a mere three kilometre (a couple of miles) long run. All my life I had been mostly a water-based athlete and at that stage I had not run more than to catch the odd bus or train a few years before that day. Six months later, I finished my first full marathon very close to the gold recreational standard of four hours (hold your applause please, millions do this stuff every year). As much as the marathon training was new to me and taxing, it was a great way to prepare my body for a completely new challenge, to remind myself just how to listen to it and to activate the old and new knowledge about human movement and what happens to our bodies when we train. And just what does that have to do with a goalkeeping book and chapter on physical readiness of goalkeepers?

It's another one of the countless examples of the importance of understanding the principles behind the methods. I was completely new to long distance running but my understanding of the principles of training as a water polo goalkeeper and coach allowed me to design and adjust my own running training routine. Filtering the ocean of advice of all kinds, awareness of different energy systems that fuelled different types of training runs, appreciation of biomechanics that allowed me to run efficiently and injury free ... it all became useful in a completely different context. Paying attention to and knowing what our body does and needs is as powerful in goalkeeping as it is in marathon running.

So far in this book we have explored how, where and when to move. Let's have a look at the common ways of making sure the goalkeepers are physically fit enough to do so and do it well. Just like the rest of the book, this is about the principles that cut across sports, not the methods in each of them.

You don't have to be an elite goalkeeping brain to realise that goalkeepers need three basic physical attributes, regardless of their body build and level of experience. Firstly, they need to be able to move fast in multiple directions. Being strong is of course an advantage to prevent injuries, make firmer saves, distribute the ball further and more. But the ability to move the body and limbs fast and with a high degree of coordination and control is crucial. Secondly, goalkeepers need to be able to generate and sustain short periods of intense, maximum effort work. Goalkeeping is not a steady marathon but a series of sometimes almost maniacal bursts of effort which goalkeepers need to produce and sustain for relatively short amounts of time compared to the field players. Thirdly, goalkeepers also need to have a good general fitness 'base'. This allows them to stay focused and produce exactly the same intensity and speed of movement in the first, last or any minute of the game, tournament or season when these may be decided. The field players may get tired as the effects of constant movement and contact take their toll, the goalkeepers must not. Let's have a look at these three attributes more closely.[30]

Whatever the sport, goalkeepers need to be able to 'explode' in an instant, like a coiled spring. I have used the analogy of goalkeepers moving like cats before and if you have ever seen a cat pounce from its spot you can visualise that one again. Goalkeepers need to be able to generate that cat-like 'explosive power'. It's a good way to describe this type of force but the terms 'explosive' and 'power' get thrown around a lot and need a brief clarification.[31]

What is *power*? First, it is *not* the same as strength. Put simply, both terms refer to the force upon an object, but *strength* is to resist and *power* is to move something. Then there is also a difference in the dimension of time. Mathematically, power equals force times distance over time ($P = F \times D/t$). The shorter the time to generate the same amount of force the more powerful, not stronger, the goalkeeper is. The term *explosive* refers to the ability not only to react and to move fast but to move, in the language of physiologists, with 'maximal velocity' in the shortest amount of time. In practical terms, to stop the fastest of shots, it's not enough for the goalkeeper to act fast. They also need to be able to move as fast as possible as soon as possible. We saw in chapter 4 how and why this ability is likely to be even more prominent as shot speeds continue to challenge the limits of basic human reaction.

Explosive power can be developed in a combination of two ways - by developing strength to increase the force and by developing speed to decrease the movement time. Getting physically stronger definitely helps. With appropriate training, not only the muscles but the tendons (attachment of muscles to bones and other structures), the ligaments (attachment of bone to bone) and bones themselves[32] get stronger to enable and support the increased ability to generate force and sustain the training for it. But because goalkeepers are not rugby forwards who need to increase what TV commentators and pundits call 'pure strength' to block bodies and push the opposition out of the way, development of 'pure speed' is more prominent in working with goalkeepers.

Goalkeepers across sports will be familiar with dynamic and/ or ballistic movements in training where they are forced to move their body as fast they can. Sometimes they do so with weights or some other form of resistance to overcome the comfortable and unconsciously learned 'speed barrier' of their movement. If you have ever done a movement with even a small weight, then took it off and performed the same movement you'll know not just what this is but also what it feels like.

I am going to resist getting (too) technical here and simply invite you to explore this fascinating field further. What I feel is important to note though is that this commonly called 'speed' is partly genetic and partly developmental. Some peoples' muscle fibres are simply built to their advantage, some people respond well to training their explosive power and some less so. Ideally, training would take account of the goalkeeper's genetics and consider what they have and what they can develop. It is prudent to recognise and nurture what is genetically gifted, develop what can be developed and not lament something a goalkeeper has not been born with[33]. It is essential to work on goalkeepers' speed to give them a chance of improvement but blaming them for 'not working hard enough' in improving something they may be physically unable to improve is silly at best and demoralising at worst. Don't give up too quickly either! Improvements in speed take much longer than for example improvements in endurance or aerobic capacity.

Let's now look at the other two physiological attributes mentioned as key to goalkeeping. At the risk of pointing out the obvious, no sport requires goalkeepers to sustain constant movement and lengthy bouts of endurance like most field players. What goalkeepers in all sports do require however is to generate and sustain high intensity efforts for relatively shorter bouts compared to their teammates in the field. Most of this workload comes from the actions to get into and/or maintain the most optimal position from which they can then intervene with the final burst to stop or prevent shots. The amount of time goalkeepers spend in this highly alert and highly active zone can vary greatly between sports and within the sports themselves. This depends on the type of play, defensive structures and more. Generally, these are bouts of high activity between a few up and up to 60 seconds, allowing for exceptions of course. In the vernacular, this is where goalkeepers 'go nuts', 'work their butt off', 'stay sharp', 'get in the zone' ... They are followed by recovery phases and a significant drop in physical exertion and with it the goalkeepers' heart rate.

To perform their feats, goalkeepers use three basic energy systems. In this they are no different to the field players or any other human being for that matter. What differs is the ratio of using each energy system compared to the field players. While there are a number of useful studies[34] that look at specific use of different energy systems by goalkeepers in different sports, it would be pointless to try to accurately quantify the ratios of use of each energy system *across* different sports here. This is because they may vary not just between the sports but within the sports, even single games by the same goalkeeper. So sorry, no detailed percentage breakdown here but for the purpose of this text, let us establish that during games goalkeepers use mostly the aerobic system but rely heavily on two anaerobic systems (phosphate and lactic) during the crucial positioning and interventions.

What are these three energy systems? Just a brief physiological summary here, there are of course variations and further sub-systems. Energy for any activity in the muscles is provided by a complex organic chemical called adenosine triphosphate (ATP). This is the 'currency of life'. The trouble with ATP is that at any time we only have a small amount of it stored in our muscles. During an activity, it needs to be constantly replenished from other fuel sources either with the help of oxygen (aerobic) and without it (anaerobic), as shown by the diagram overleaf.

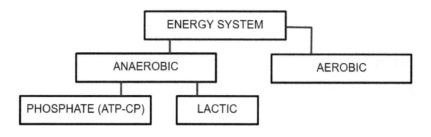

Image adapted from Pyke, 1999

In the ATP-CP (*Phosphate*) phase, the small amount of ATP and another high energy substance called creatine phosphate (CP) stored in our muscles provide enough energy for short bursts of activity up to approximately 10 seconds, even less for maximum efforts. Goalkeepers use this system just about any time they produce a quick dash, move, sudden jump, lunge or similar action. What is really cool about this energy system is that these energy stores are quickly rebuilt. After only 30 seconds of rest, half of this energy is available again and completely restored within a couple of minutes. Staple of goalkeeping!

When an intense effort continues beyond the limits of the phosphate system, glycogen (a type of sugar) stored in the muscle kicks in as the supply of ATP. Maximum or close to maximum efforts up to about two minutes demand a lot of energy quickly. This process happens without the help of oxygen (*anaerobic*). But while it can provide great amounts of energy fast, this process also creates a lot of *lactic* acid. The rapid loss of glycogen and the buildup of lactic acid that we can't clear fast enough cause us to fatigue out. Anytime goalkeepers' heart rate and breathing spike out dramatically during the intense and prolonged bouts of hard work in the goalmouth, they dip into this anaerobic lactic energy system. While goalkeepers certainly use it, it is definitely not to the acute, repeated exhaustion levels as the field players from which it may take up to 60 minutes to fully recover. Replacing a goalkeeper during a game because of the level of tiredness that significantly affects their performance would have to be extremely rare in any sport.

For the vast majority of their game time, goalkeepers use the aerobic energy system. In this case, oxygen is used to release energy from the glycogen and fat stored in the muscle to supply ATP. During low intensity efforts that we could 'do all day', glycogen stores deplete much slower and the small amount of lactic acid created is easily cleared. While the values across sports may differ, things like standing, walking, jogging, floating and similar activities performed while watching and/or directing play take up the biggest part of goalkeepers' time during the game.

Sure, these are all pretty easy but goalkeepers need a solid base of aerobic fitness to perform them whenever required and equally well throughout the game, tournament or season. Without that, the concentration may lapse, the faster, energy-sapping anaerobic system might kick in earlier and more.

Why all this talk of energy systems, ratios and chemicals? Very few of us are finely tuned elite performing goalkeeping specimens so do we really need to know this? Well, by now we have established that goalkeepers are an important part of the team and that they are in so many ways different to the field players. But just how different should goalkeepers' physical training be then compared to other team members? After all, there are other specialists in a team that hone their particular skills. Attackers practice their shots more, centre backs their defensive moves - why are the goalkeepers so special?

Well, goalkeepers don't just use a few different sets of skills like attackers or defenders. They use *entire energy systems* very differently compared to the field players. Imagine you are a running coach. Sure, your sprinters may have some long runs but chances are you wouldn't slap them constantly with marathoner's mileage in training and vice versa. As for the answer to "how different (the training should be)?", the best immediate answer would probably be "it depends" and take it from there, whatever your sport. But please do consider the differences in goalkeepers' energy and endurance demands.

The other important thing to consider is that apart from the very extremes, all three energy systems are used, to different extent of course, just about all the time, not just when we decide to focus on improving a specific one of them in training. For example, light drills with speed and technique work may be using the same ratios of energy system use as miles and miles of what may be boring light jogging or swimming intended to 'develop the aerobic energy system'. Training in goals using challenging drills, games or repeated realistic scenarios builds both the specificity of muscle movement, spatial awareness, reaction, anticipation (things talked about in chapters 3 and 4) as well as the same energy systems as a bunch of generic '10 x 100s'. No, I am not dismissing goalkeepers doing 'boring sets' here. The biggest advantage of such sets, physiological at least, is that we can pinpoint almost exactly the type and the extent of a particular energy system taxed and strengthened. It is however useful to understand the bigger picture of the goalkeeper. It is prudent to know what energy systems are we training/taxing more or less with different activities and the opportunity cost of it all, expressed in a question "at the expense of what (are we doing this)?"

What about strength training in the gym? The place that water polo players call 'dry land'. There have and will continue to be endless discussions about what goalkeepers should do there. More weights, less weights, higher reps, weightlifting, bands, plyometrics … It is again very tempting to unload a pile of well-known training methods and their pros and cons. If you are a coach I will get you to do that yourself, making sure you are doing the right thing by your goalkeepers by making them fitter and faster without injuring them. But what has emerged from my conversations with goalkeepers and their coaches in different sports is the importance of developing agility and a strong core.

I have already mentioned in chapter 3 what agility is and why it is important. I won't labour the point here other than to remind that agility refers to a combination of reflexes, coordination, balance and speed that enables the goalkeeper to move and change direction in a controlled and adequate way. Agile means being able to act and adjust quickly and efficiently. But as important as this ability is, it is severely impoverished without the second key aspect that can be developed with strength training.

It may have been overused but I always liked the saying "you can't shoot a cannon out of a canoe" (check YouTube for the literal and funny efforts though). Any momentum generated will be diminished without a strong, firm base to act from. This is basic physics, Newton's third law of action equal to reaction. Agility - great. Strong and fast legs to get yourself in a position - great. But what is equally or perhaps even more important is a strong set of 'core muscles' to act *from*. No, this is not the outer abdominal 'six pack' layer, as sexy as it may look. The *core* refers to the group of deep, inner muscles wrapping around and controlling our pelvis and spine. A mountain of research, and a mountain of common sense, confirms that a strong core enables faster and more efficient movement and at the same time reduces the risk of injury. Just about any movement by a goalkeeper, from getting in the position and balancing their centre of gravity to interventions and more is affected by their core. The crowd might see the goalkeeper's arms flying through the air to reach the ball but they can't see the very important base from which this movement is supported and launched from.

From body weight, apparatus and weight assisted to yoga and more ... there are plenty of ways to strengthen the core. Sometimes the trouble with exercising the core is that it is simply assumed and/or deliberately skipped to focus on something that is more visible and immediate. At goalkeeper's peril! Like many of my fellow goalkeepers, I sadly learned this lesson the hard way. I injured my back in a twisting move mere five minutes into playing in the world championship I had trained months and months for. Strengthening my core, not my back, not only fixed my back but also made me a better goalkeeper later on.

But physical preparation is more than making sure goalkeepers are able to move and last the game. It is also about making sure they have a good technique to move well enough to do the job. By 'good technique' I mean a desired movement performed consistently that fits the goalkeeper's physique and follows sound biomechanical principles.

Technique work is another fertile ground for theories and approaches, agreements and disagreements. While there certainly are some sensible and less sensible approaches, it may not be a good idea to endorse one overall as the gospel. Why? Every goalkeeper is different, subtly or markedly so. This is perfectly fine, even desirable as it allows us to have different strengths too.

Some goalkeepers are simply more 'active', almost fidgety, and need to be that way to do their job best. Some are cool as ice without an extra movement in sight, some look heavy or 'lazy' but somehow get to the ball and more. Ideally, we would work out which of the goalkeeper's movements to leave alone, which to correct and which to eliminate. Good news? No one was born with such an ability to work it out, it can only be developed.

Video and analytical tools, many of them at very low cost, can be very helpful here but no tool can tell us what to look for and how to make sense of it. Deciding what to do with different technical aspects is best informed by knowing the reasons for working on them in the first place. Take for example a football goalkeeper who regularly loses precious milliseconds by first moving their hands even slightly inward to protect the body before moving towards the ball. The reason for it is likely the fear of getting hit. You can hammer them on improving technique but without addressing the underlying fear, that technical improvement you want to see may take a lot more time and energy.

When it comes to technique work, there is one important 'do not' that myself and many other coaches in different sports I have spoken to in writing this book agree on - don't just 'let technique happen' with no deliberate thought, practice and feedback.

You may know a lot about technique, spend a lot of time working on it as a goalkeeper or a coach and you are perhaps really fond of a particular way of goalkeeping. On the other side, you may have very little idea or perhaps you are unsure of your knowledge of goalkeeping technique in your sport. No matter where you are on this continuum, there are a few questions that you can never waste asking, as a goalkeeper or their coach.

Start perhaps with "Does the technique used allow this goalkeeper to play well enough *with the current level of fitness*?" While it is rarely so clear cut, if fitness is the main issue - work on that and get them fit as best you can. If the goalkeeper is fit enough and mentally OK but not doing well in a particular aspect of the game (for example, difficulty stopping certain types of shots) try the next question: "Is the goalkeeper doing things that make sense in terms of basic physics and biomechanics?"

If the goalkeeper is doing something that goes completely against the basic biomechanical principles and simply compensating for it, even quite successfully so, it may be worth exploring further. Ever seen a goalkeeper that sits so far forward or back that their centre of gravity (see chapter 3) is hard to just maintain let alone move and adjust quickly? What about a goalkeeper who shortens their reach and loses the sight of the ball by regularly turning their head away from it? We're not talking about minute tweaks of their little pinky finger but fundamentals. Making changes to fundamentals may seem a little strange, laboured at first. It will probably cost a few more goals in training as the goalkeeper may simply not be used to it at first. Once a correction to obey the unbending laws of physics in the basic, most repeated movements and positions (for example, the basic stance, 'poise' in goals) is internalised and adjusted to, it does not guarantee success but certainly increases the goalkeeper's chances of it. What's more, it allows innovation with the security of knowing we're not cheating the science, only building on it to improve.

Sure, there may be some exceptional goalkeepers with 'freakish' ability that seemingly defy such laws as if by magic. But it's no magic. They have or are doing something that gives them the biomechanical edge. Quite possibly they may not even be aware of or responsible for it! It could be the extra flexibility in a particular joint or two, particularly high percentage of the fast twitch muscle fibres, extraordinary foot speed or something else that makes them look super human and as such close to impossible to copy by someone else. This leads to the next question: "Is the goalkeeper doing things they look and are comfortable doing given their age and build?"

Chances are once their technique makes sense in terms of basic physics, goalkeepers actually look and feel more comfortable. It is simply easier to move! This is where juniors start to look like the more experienced adults, even if in glimpses. Of course they will be inconsistent at first but the sooner a junior does what a technically good adult would do the better. Once they grow and strengthen, the neural paths to perform the movements faster and more competently will be there already to meet the new found strength. While there certainly are steps and milestones of progression at different stages of development, no goalkeeper or coach from across different sports I spoke to said there is a 'junior technique' to teach before 'adult technique'.

This of course does *not* mean that we should expect and demand that a 12 year old move like a pro on TV straight away! Their bodies, strength, knowledge and experiences are not only partially developed but may be very different to their (or your?) goalkeeping idol. It is great to have idols and role models (see the entire chapter dedicated to this very issue) but there are so many other factors at play that make producing a mirror image of a particular adult very problematic. Young goalkeepers learning the sound basics of technique they can use now and later as adults is essential. Trying to be an adult or carbon copying one especially when very young is unrealistic and possibly very damaging.

Some goalkeepers may have good biomechanical basics, even look and feel comfortable for their age and body type but they keep getting injured. This begs the next question: "Is the goalkeeper doing things that are more likely to get them injured?" No, we are not talking about the determination to get in the way of limb and ball required by goalkeepers (see next chapters on that). We are talking about goalkeepers moving their body repeatedly in ways that may not cope well with various forces. For example, I have seen too many water polo goalkeepers who try to slap and/or stop the ball behind their shoulders instead of in line with or in front of shoulders and later wonder why they keep getting painful hyper-extended elbows. Take a video, then zoom in and slow-motion the moment the ball hits the arm. Ouch! Injuries, especially the acute, repeated ones, may be the common signal of a problem here. Hopefully, we can prevent or mitigate the effects of injuries with a timely change in the technique and/or training, then allow time for it to become that automated, natural movement.

But let's say the goalkeeper plays well with good basics, they are comfortable in their body, have no repeat injuries ... is there more to technique? Of course there is - but at the expense of what? Even when technique is established, constant work on it is necessary to bury it further to the automated, subconscious level. Remember the previous chapter and the Bruce Lee 10,000 kicks quote at the end of it? Technique can be tweaked of course, but you would be wise to ask yourself if the (over)tweaking is worth the goalkeeper's confidence in their ability to work with the strengths they have. This is especially important if they are a more mature goalkeeper and/or very close to an important event. At the same time, it is neither kind nor wise to leave young goal-keepers to their own devices, then spending many hours correcting the most basic aspects when they mature and such a thing becomes increasingly disruptive and difficult, rather than laying down the sound basics early. Before changing technique, ask and honestly answer three questions:

- Is the change *necessary* (and why)?
- Is the change *reasonable* (and why)?
- Is the time and effort (to be) spent on the change *proportionate* with the advantage gained or problem avoided, now and in the future?

I close this chapter on physical preparation and technical development with three interconnected messages to three very important groups of people.

To parents, supporters and anyone else interested in goalkeepers, especially young ones - be patient. Each human body is unique, amazing and can do magnificent things but it changes all the time, whether we like it or not.

To goalkeepers - know your body, how it works, where it is at and what it needs to play your best at different stages of your goalkeeping career.

To coaches - what your goalkeeper *needs* is always more important than what *you know*.

'All In The Head' by Sebastian Lasic

6

Inside goalkeeper's head

"Look, there's the man who made all of Brazil cry!"

These were the words of a mother to her young son upon seeing Moacir Barbosa in a shop in 1970, 20 years after the final game of the 1950 football World Cup in Brazil where the host nation shockingly lost to Uruguay 2-1. Barbosa had a great tournament and was voted goalkeeper of the tournament. At 1-1 and eleven minutes left in the final game, he let in a shot he would have saved a hundred times before. He logically anticipated a cross from an advancing winger with a poor angle but Ghiggia actually mishit the ball and the ball bobbled through past the near post. Barbosa's fate was sealed and what followed is a sad story of a man who died in poverty fifty years after what was to be his own, his team's and his country's crowning achievement. "Under Brazilian law the maximum sentence is 30 years. But my imprisonment has been for 50 years" were his words not long before he died. Barbosa's story is probably one of the most dramatic ones among the thousands that show how the gift of the decider that goalkeepers have can easily turn into a haunting curse. On the other hand, there are also thousands of stories of goalkeepers using this gift to overcome the odds and inspire others in their team and beyond.

Goalkeeping is a physically and particularly mentally intense activity for many of the reasons discussed so far in this book. On one side, there is the intense focus required to read the play and track the ball, the single-minded courage required to get in harm's way and the potential to dash the hopes and undo all the hard work of teammates and fans with a single slip up, real or perceived as Barbosa would tell you. On the other side is the limelight, the attention, the power to lead the team and perhaps heroically decide the winner. Both sides take their toll as the highs are high and the lows are low. History is replete with goalkeepers whose flamboyance and supreme confidence were followed by bouts of self-doubt, poor mental health and even suicide[35]. Let's look inside that complex space - the goal-keeper's head.

To start, let's get right into the game! Each game has its spikes of physical activity and focus for the goalkeeper. Each game can also be won or lost, made or marred by a goalkeeper in a flash. For this reason, goalkeepers have to maintain their focus and stay alert throughout the game. Awake, fully present, aware of primarily oneself, surrounds and the flow of the game. They might have looked jobless but several football and field hockey goalkeepers I spoke with described their exhaustion and "socks dripping in sweat" after games where they barely had to make a save, but focused intensely on the ball and play while thinking, directing, preventing, anticipating, and making calls for the entire game. This alert state is amplified in sports with relatively smaller fields where transition of play from one end to another can regularly take just a few seconds (for example ice hockey, futsal, handball). Switching off at any time during the game is very dangerous. Search for 'funny goalkeeper mistakes' on YouTube and you will see the consequences of it. After the game, switching off is desirable but can be difficult while reliving the glorious saves, thinking of plays or brooding over a mistake or a poor game.

Approaching opposition elevates goalkeeper's arousal in the form of sometimes very strong emotions and responses. They may be nervous for what is to come if unprepared, surprised by a sudden development, welcoming the upcoming contest, angry at the way their team lost the ball in attack and more. When the opposition bears down, 'it gets personal' as some goalkeepers put it.

After the intense bouts of activity in front of the goals, the play moves up the field and goalkeepers may 'power down' their arousal but ideally stay in the 'zone of optimal arousal'. This is a well-known concept in the psychology of human performance and perhaps best shown with the diagram overleaf.

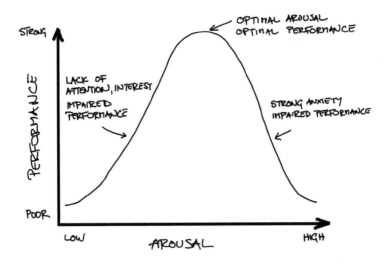

This curve is a common and useful way of showing what happens not just during a game but also before and after it. Hanin[36] expanded on this model and proposed that we react differently to arousal based on our emotions, personality and level of expertise. One of the biggest insights of his research is that rather than distinguishing between 'positive' and 'negative' emotional states, it is more useful to classify them as helpful (optimal) and unhelpful (dysfunctional) to each individual. For example, some goalkeepers may find excitement unhelpful while others could not perform without it. Others may do their best work in the cage when angry while the same emotion would be a killer for another goalkeeper.

Hanin also proposed that we consider Individual Zones of Optimal Functioning (IZOF)[37] for the amount of arousal each athlete needs to perform at the best.[38] In our case, some goalkeepers may need low and others high levels of arousal to do so, as illustrated by the figure overleaf.

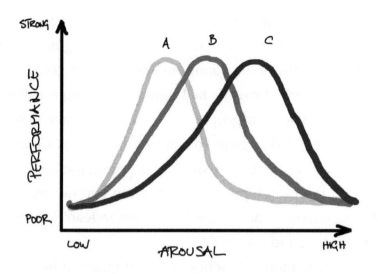

In this case, Goalkeeper A has a low IZOF and too much arousal for them would lead to suboptimal performance. At the other end, Goalkeeper C needs high levels of arousal (high IZOF) to perform best. They would be underperforming at the levels of arousal that suit Goalkeeper A and even, to a lesser extent, Goalkeeper B.

This is important to consider for two key reasons. One is that each goalkeeper would be well advised to spend some time reflecting on what arousal state gets them performing best. Having the awareness of emotions and levels of arousal allows for the possibility of a goalkeeper to manage those emotions and self regulate. Self regulation improves the chances of achieving and maintaining the optimal level of arousal. Secondly, recognising the uniqueness of each goalkeeper when coaching them is more likely to produce better outcomes than expecting, even demanding that *all* goalkeepers be like raging bulls, emotionless machines or something else in between. Such demands are usually borne out of coaches' own experiences as a goalkeeper ('it worked for me') and/or ways that one imagines an 'ideal' goalkeeper should look, sound and feel like. It could end up being the proverbial road to hell paved with good intentions.

Next time you hear people say "you would have to be crazy to go in goals" I challenge you to ask them why. Chances are the main reasons for their sentiment go along the lines of '(not) getting hurt' and 'the pressure to perform and not make costly mistakes'. Often we hear these two common fears referred to as a fear of injury and a fear of failure.

'Fear' is an emotion that lies on a continuum of intensity. For example, a goalkeeper may be anywhere from a little nervous before or during a game, worried about, to perhaps absolutely overwhelmed and paralysed in fear of making a mistake. The intensity may change, sometimes in a moment, but the under-lying emotion is the same, as either anticipation of a threat or immediate response to it.

What may also change is the length of the feeling. The niggling nerves may quickly fade. On the other side of the continuum, a goalkeeper could be 'stuck' in a particular emotion and it may become a chronic, ongoing impediment on their learning and performance. This is often labelled as anxiety[39]. Anxiety is not a feeling but an umbrella term for a range of feelings, thoughts and bodily experiences associated with the way we respond to fears[40]. For natural worriers, anxiety is a *trait* of their personality but we may all be in an anxious *state* at times.

In-depth definitions and discussion of terms like fear and anxiety are much beyond the scope of this book[41]. But just like knowing that goalkeepers may have different optimal arousal levels, recognising that fear and anxiety have different forms, intensities, lengths and ways in which they affect different goalkeepers is useful. Trying to clear up what exactly are we dealing with is the first step to managing emotional states in order to get what each individual goalkeeper needs to stay healthy and operate at their best.

Athletes in any position or sport often experience certain fears and anxieties due to the nature, demands and expectations of their sport. Fears of injury and failure are not the only ones nor are they somehow unique to goalkeepers. However, their prevalence among goalkeepers makes them worthy of having a closer look at. I think I am getting a few nods from fellow goalkeepers here.

Being a goalkeeper requires the courage to get in harm's way. A well struck or thrown projectile flying towards you at great speed or a body part in fast motion can hurt a great deal, especially if hitting an exposed or poorly protected body area. Like my fellow water polo goalkeepers, I know the feeling of half a kilo of wet rubber travelling from a few metres away at just under 100km/h smashing into my face or bouncing off the post and hitting my outstretched fingers at a right angle. Handball or futsal goalkeepers have to endure an even faster meeting of leather and their body, not to mention the 'mad'[42] goalkeepers in hurling facing a small, hard *sliotar* that would regularly clock over 100km/h with nothing but a face mask and a hurl that looks like a small wooden paddle. In some sports, the goalkeeper needs to move towards attackers at full speed right in the path of a likely collision. Sticking their hands and face in front of a sprinting attacker to grab the ball they are desperately trying to kick is a known specialty of football goalkeepers. So are their dives and thumping landings on the ground from sometimes several feet above ground.

All of the above can and does hurt. Most of the general population would instinctively wince or move to avoid the pain. Anxiety about it seems perfectly normal as a protective response to the potential danger to our body. Getting hurt may confirm the validity of such anxiety, something along the lines of "I had been worried about getting hurt and I did get hurt. As a result I will avoid getting hurt!" Yet goalkeepers are expected to not just endure but actively suffer likely pain if it means protecting the net. Only in the youngest juniors would a goalkeeper get away with letting in the goal because 'it may hurt' to get in the way. Anxiety about getting hurt at any level may cause substandard performance by avoiding the danger (ball strike, body collision) that would lead to anxiety about failure ... I'm sure you get the vicious circle.

What about performance anxiety? Goalkeepers are human. Flesh and blood. No matter how confident or skilled they are, goalkeepers also can and *do* make mistakes and fail sometimes. Games, careers, fortunes of not just individuals but entire clubs or national teams have turned on the fortunes, skill and sometimes a momentary lapse by a goalkeeper. Performance anxiety is of course not limited to goalkeepers. There have been thousands of examples of other skilled athletes who 'couldn't handle it' and have either fumbled, choked or somehow else failed to perform to the standard required on a particularly important and/or tense occasion. However, goalkeepers are playing in a key position and one that is easy to find fault and blame in by a generally unskilled eye of the public. Common word for what this sort of thing breeds? Pressure.

High stakes of the match, expectations of fans, media, family, friends, club, historical rivalry and more are just some of the many factors external to the goalkeeper that can ratchet up the pressure to perform well on a particular occasion. Add to this goalkeeper's own expectations and the anxiety can shoot up and take the goalkeeper out of their zone of optimal arousal. This is where the heart races, hands shake, legs turn to lead and head wanders to unhelpful places that stymie performance. The burden of expectations often gives rise to an old and well-known companion that goalkeepers use to deal with, minimise or perhaps even avoid pressure, real and/or perceived[43] - perfectionism.

The small margins of error; the lack of safety net in case of mistakes; the different set of expectations of the amount of acceptable errors compared to field players; the ephemeral nature of saves versus the permanency of goals conceded and recorded for posterity; the ease of scrutiny by people who may have little or no knowledge of the game; the increased scrutiny afforded by the development of recording technology to spot and magnify goalkeeper's weaknesses or howlers; the fierce competition for a single position with no alternative; the increasing ease of social media to spread the glorious acts and embarrassing moments worldwide at great speed and more … No wonder that goalkeepers across sports are likely to show increased perfectionist tendencies in their training, game and possibly private life.

Perfectionism is a strategy, and certainly not the only one, to prevent unhelpful anxiety. Setting high standards of excellence and expectations is honourable and indeed desirable. But when these become unrealistic, a nice-sounding precept like "get it perfect and you will have nothing to worry about" can become a curse for several reasons goalkeepers will be familiar with.

Firstly, mistakes and setbacks *will* happen, no matter what the skill, experience, team, support or other factors. Sport, and especially team sport, is too dynamic to expect that everything will go our way. Expecting everything and everyone, including oneself, to be and act perfectly in line with our expectations is an incredibly unrealistic, naive, toddler-like view of the self and the world. Secondly, if nothing but perfection is good enough, goalkeepers may begin ignoring the positives from the 'less than perfect' while never matching their own, potentially unrealistic, expectations. The expected future 'perfect' makes the achieved and often joyful, sustaining 'good enough' now invisible, almost its enemy. Thirdly, because goalkeepers' imperfections and mistakes are often eas(iest) to point out and blame for a loss or poor performance by others, the goalkeepers themselves may fall for 'goalies' blame', believing their actions alone 'lost the game'. Never mind the missed opportunities of strikers, lost balls, dangerous passes, poor tactics and a myriad of other actions that would have contributed to the loss ... "it's the goalkeeper's fault"! All these can trigger a vicious cycle of under-performance, unhelpful (self)blame and anxiety about it(self)!

A list of possible anxieties for goalkeepers is too long to attempt let alone exhaust here. But there is one more source of it that is worth mentioning as it seems quite prominent among goalkeepers. Field players are often played in different and multiple roles, especially at junior levels. As they develop and specialise playing in preferred roles, the range of options for them decreases but there is still some scope to move them around, try them in a different role, use them more sparingly, tweak selections and more. No such luck for the lone goalkeeper! There is only ever one single playing spot for a goalkeeper, as written in the rules of a sport with one. Unless agreed to before the game, tournament or season, the unwritten rules of most sports also make changing a goalkeeper during a game a rarity in most sports (some sports have tactical exemptions, for example handball). With goalkeepers generally training together, it is hard, let's admit it, to watch your training partner do what you have both trained for while you keep the bench warm[44], sometimes for long streaks of games. At selection times, this may intensify and the many weeks, months or even years of work end up pitting one goalkeeper against another for that sole spot. Missing out and/or sitting out breeds disappointment and sometimes resentment against others or it is turned inward to the self.

In chapter 2 I mentioned that for many out there goalkeeping is more than a playing position. It is a part of their identity, of who they are. Success in goals or lack of it lifts them or drags them down not just on but also off the field. It affects their self-esteem, the feeling of worth for who they are not (just) as a goalkeeper but a person. I acknowledge that separation of the 'goalkeeper' from 'me' can be very difficult but sometimes this could be a game, career or even life saving distinction to make for the sake of mental health *and* better performance. Feeling that you are a perfectly normal, acceptable human being despite all the glory and/or the mistakes made in goals is a lot healthier than feeling that what you do in goals defines you not just as a goalkeeper but as a person. Despite the best intentions, learning to recognise and acknowledge the distinction between human *doing* and human *being* may sometimes be beyond the knowledge or skill of a goalkeeper, teammates or their coach. In such cases I would strongly recommend seeking professional psychological help.

So far, this chapter has hardly been an advertisement for goalkeeping. Is it all mental doom and gloom for goalkeepers? Sure, what has been described so far are not the most pleasant mental states. But here comes the good news!

We *do* need emotions, we *can* eliminate some sources of anxiety and we *can* make some of them work *for* and not against goalkeepers. It is better to manage rather than try to shut emotions down. There needs to be a balance between emotion and rational and reasonable thought. In neurological terms, this is the balance between the 'thinking brain' (frontal cortex) and the 'emotional brain' (amygdala). For example, during a game there needs to be clear thinking to access things like strategy, game plan, knowledge of players and more. But there *also* needs to be emotion, including a degree of excitement, joy, and other emotions like fear (yes, fear!), present to motivate and energise for best performance and learning.

Fear of getting hurt may rightly stop you doing something stupid in life but it is not your friend in goals. This is one source of anxiety, especially in younger goalkeepers, that would ideally be eliminated. Learning how to move smarter, how to brace and/or protect from blows; anticipate and possibly prevent or minimise impact with timely and successful intervention; improvement in physical ability and muscle mass to cushion physical blows; age and character-appropriate, gradual desensitisation to physical impact commonly associated with goalkeeping; improved motivation to face common dangers of getting hurt in goals - these are just some of the many ways the necessary courage to perform well in goals can be developed. The natural instinct to get in the way may not be there at first but can become present and automatic through practice. You may want to perhaps ask and copy techniques used by other sports to work on this with your goalkeepers, especially from a young age. Once mastered, it not only avoids or minimises the pain but gives the impression of fearless invincibility. This forms an important part of the goalkeeper's presence, described at length in the next chapter.

How about harnessing and working with rather than trying to (hopelessly) eliminate mental pressure? Just like developing the capacity to deal with physical challenges, facing and managing initially very predictable, gradual and manageable amounts of pressure through games, drills and challenges can build emotional maturity and resilience of a goalkeeper. This can be particularly powerful if followed by regular feedback and support, suitable to the level of skill and stage of development. It stands to produce better results than overprotective lack of exposure to pressure and expectations on one side or a blunt 'sink or swim' or perhaps hyper-achieving aspiration on the other for goalkeepers at all levels, not just juniors. Excuse pointing out the obvious here but the best way to learn how to handle pressure is by … handling the appropriate amount of pressure.

Anxiety can actually be a source of strength and small amounts of it are perfectly normal, useful, necessary even in our lives. It energises us to plan, organise, discipline and act better than just 'going with the flow'. It gets us into that sweet spot of arousal where we are vigilant and at our best to engage with the challenge at hand. Because of this we would ideally aim not to eliminate it but to find the optimal amount of anxiety each goalkeeper needs to operate at their best, as suggested by Hanin's IZOF model mentioned earlier.

As for perfectionism - it's not all bad, far from it. Strong work ethic, high expectations and attention to detail are all common features of a perfectionist. They are all also not just highly sought but essential qualities of a goalkeeper or athlete of any kind for that matter. But there is a catch! When healthy and realistic, these qualities work *for* the goalkeeper. When excessive and wildly unrealistic, they work *against* and could even ruin the goalkeeper.

What is also a lot healthier and more useful is a focus on the process rather than the outcome. It is no good in keeping 'eyes on the prize' if it takes our eyes off what we need to do to get there. Focusing on doing well the things that we *can* do now is a very different thing to obsessive expectation of a perfect future outcome. Clean sheets, team selections, perfect attempts, records, national team glory or a big professional contract are great to dream about and aspire to. But if these are not likely matched by the realities of the goalkeeper's ability and/or achievement they can (and often do!) kill the joy of goalkeeping and sport at large even. While they can be enormously motivating, hopes and dreams are exactly that - we may have them but we are *not* in charge of them. Goals, ideally, are something very different and consist of things that we are in charge of and are realistically achievable. Confusing dreams and goals as the same thing can be very dangerous.

I once heard a wonderful story of a coach of a junior team who slipped a note under the hotel room door of all players on the morning of their tournament final with a quote: "It is OK to have butterflies in your stomach. Now let's get them to fly in formation." They did just that and won the game. And just how *do* we get those butterflies to fly in formation? Confidence?

'Confidence' is a term we commonly use to describe one's strong belief to achieve a goal they set out to achieve. "Winners do not doubt and doubters do not win" was one of the dictums of Gerry Ehrmann, a famous producer of a line of outstanding German football goalkeepers in his *Flugschule* in Kaiserslautern.[45] How about mottoes like "Believe in yourself and you can do anything!" screaming from motivational posters. Add motivation, technically 'a desire to succeed', and you have the stuff of Hollywood scenarios. But as glorious as this combo may sound - it may not be enough! It needs to be *legitimate*. What exactly are we confident and motivated about? What makes us feel, know, say so? There is perhaps a more useful and accurate concept to describe what gets us to make confidence and pressure dance together.

According to Albert Bandura, who coined the term[46], self-efficacy is the "belief in one's capabilities to execute behaviours necessary to produce a specific level of performance attainments." In other words, you will do best when you back yourself and believe that you are able to succeed and/or persist at a particular task at a particular time with what you have and are capable of. Bandura identified four separate but highly inter-related sources or ways of generating high levels of self-efficacy[47], *italicised* below. The aim here is not to discuss these sources of self-efficacy in great depth but simply name them and show what they likely look like in the context of goalkeeping so they can be considered in working with goalkeepers.

Performance accomplishments such as mastering a skill or playing well raise the level of belief in the goalkeeper's own ability and their motivation to do it again. Thousands of high quality repeats of a skill that lead to perfect and almost unconscious execution every time, a string of consistently good saves and games, visualised action that unfolds exactly as imagined, the feeling of 'reading the game' are just a few examples goalkeepers can relate to. Success breeds success in a positive spiral, lack of it a possible downward spiral of disappointment and giving up.

We also develop self-efficacy from the second-hand, *vicarious experiences*. Most commonly this would be seeing someone modelling a particular skill or a task and/or perform it well. This is particularly powerful if the observed person is of similar skill level. With goalkeepers working together, it's the old feeling of "if they can do this, so can I..." It is a lot easier working with coaches, peers, or role models than without them. This is why having idols and role models is so important, a theme expanded on in chapter 8.

Social or *verbal persuasion* in the form of feedback and encouragement by coaches, teammates or others is another way to elevate goalkeeper's self-efficacy. We are more likely to improve our capabilities to do the job if somebody believes in us and tells us so. This includes self-talk, a common companion of goalkeepers. When believed, "you can do this" can be four incredibly powerful words. When not believed or perhaps not even uttered in the first place? You guessed it.

Lastly, our self-efficacy depends greatly on the *physiological and emotional state* we are in. We see our abilities and faults differently whether we are tired, upset, happy, anxious or something else. Making judgements about our performance and ability may be very different in the heat of the moment than later on when the heads cool down.

What about self-efficacy when things don't go well and those butterflies in our stomach lose the formation? Goalkeepers with high levels of self-efficacy are more likely to bounce back and recover from a setback than those with lower levels of self-efficacy. Work on minimising failure is of course essential but acceptance of it is prudent. Accepting failure and backing their capacity to bounce back from a setback gets champion teams and individuals (back) into that virtuous cycle of high self-efficacy and better performance. Yes, mistakes and even howlers[48] that matter will happen. What matters even more is what the goalkeeper does when they do. Perhaps perversely, people who watch sport like seeing dramatic failures. What they like even more is a comeback. High self-efficacy, belief not (just) in oneself but in one's capacity and skill to do the job *is* the fuel for it.

Goalkeepers' heads may be complex spaces but they certainly can be put to good use (primarily the insides, not just the outsides). Using the constant mental focus and managing, even thriving from the emotional states that many people would find unpalatable and seek to avoid, is an important power of goalkeepers. The key lies in 'knowing thyself'[49] – figure out what gets you to do your best, realise what you can and can't control before, during and after the games to *play* well and accept yourself no matter what so you can *be* well.

While he certainly didn't have goalkeepers in mind when writing it, the Greek Stoic philosopher Epictetus captured beautifully what to constantly remind goalkeepers of: *Just keep in mind - the more we value things outside our control, the less control we have.*

'Lift' by Sebastian Lasic

7

The Presence

"It is of huge importance to me that my opponents are intimidated by my presence between the posts. It does not matter whether it's a striker who has broken through alone to face me in a one-on-one situation or the midfielder lining up for a long range shot. No matter who it is, they have to know that I am prepared one hundred percent, that I am ready to do anything in my power to stop them from scoring."

Peter Schmeichel, Manchester United & Denmark goalkeeper

Ever seen a goalkeeper having an almost magical effect on their own team and the opposition? Felt that yourself? A force the effects of which can be seen but cannot be easily measured in goals, seconds and metres. A goalkeeper that affects people and commands respect not (just) because of the position they play but because of the way they look, sound and feel to others. That is presence.

Presence is an outward projection, something you emit. It is a feeling, largely unspoken and always existing in relation to others, not independently of others. You never fully 'have' presence or not, only achieve degrees of it and to different people. Two goalkeepers may have a very similar level of skills and experience but generate very different feelings in people.

And just what do goalkeepers want others to feel about them? Peeled down to the very basics, they want to inspire and reassure their team and unnerve the opposition. A dream of many a goalkeeper is to be an absolute hoodoo to the opposition and an inspiration to their team. And the nightmare? The opposition like sharks smelling blood and exploiting you while your own team abandons you, barely noticing your existence let alone helping you or listening to you there in the goalmouth.

Many years ago, our son started attending ju jitsu. In the very first lesson, the sensei asked the gathered bunch of kids what they think is the absolutely best way to win a fight. Sensei's answer "by not being in it" may have sounded a bit disappointing, even cowardly at first but then he explained. Making the opponent fear taking you on is the ultimate victory. Should the fight develop, as of course it does in team sports, observe the ancient rule at the heart of self-defence: how to achieve the maximum effect with minimum effort. In ju jitsu, judo and similar martial arts it is a stance, an attitude of not seeking or even being in a fight but knowing how to win smartly when you find yourself in one. Goalkeeping presence is hardly different - how to lift your team and intimidate the opposition when they seek a fight. This is why building a strong presence is an important part of goalkeeping. Let's look at some of the ways of establishing it.

It starts with asking the right question. "What can I do to be more prominent, visible and important?" may not be the best one. Presence is not all about being that. You could be wasting time and energy doing many things that may not work for you or they may even work against you.

For example, being brash and in opposition's face may sometimes be far less effective than calmly and effectively handling the trickiest shots and situations. Talking yourself up and telling the opposition they should be scared of you may work sometimes but is far, far less powerful than the opposition realising that by themselves. A better question, along the lines of the self-defence principle mentioned earlier, would then be "what is the minimal amount I can do to intimidate the opposition and help my team to the maximal effect?"

Number one thing to do? Crush with competence. Sure, a large physique, part naturally given, part developed through training, or even 'looking big'[50] may help intimidate and cover extra space. Sure, greater mobility of perhaps shorter goalkeepers may be an advantage. But whatever the goalkeeper's physical appearance, the capacity to competently keep the ball out of the net is the number one way to build presence between the sticks. It frustrates the attackers no end and the easier the goalkeepers make their job look like the greater the attackers' frustration. The aim is to make the shooter think, hesitate, doubt or perhaps even abandon a shot (the ultimate victory!). As pointed out in chapter 4, (over)thinking, doubt and even fear (of failure, usually) slow a goalkeeper down and affect the practised smoothness and effectiveness of their actions. Field players are no different in that when facing a competent goalkeeper that they know is ready and hard to beat. Schmeichel's quote at the start of this chapter reminds us of this feeling of a goalkeeper's resolve that is dreaded by many shooters.

A large part of this book is dedicated to developing the cornerstone of presence – the competence in goals. Understanding the role of the goalkeeper, positioning oneself well in space and time, reading the game and acting appropriately, handling and thriving on the responsibility [51], training and performing – these are all aspects of competence. Instead of repeating them here, let's look at two other key aspects in developing a presence. Both of them are directed more towards helping your own team rather than intimidating the opposition but they are essential aspects of a goalkeepers' presence and ways of establishing it - communication and leadership.

In writing this book, I asked field players from a range of sports "what sort of communication with your goalkeeper helps you play better?" I expected many of these answers as I have both said and heard them first hand playing in goals in different sports. Seemingly universally, in the heat of the game field players want their goalkeeper to use short, succinct, directional language. Short, specific calls like 'left', 'middle', 'drop' and similar are better than the more ambiguous 'watch it', 'careful', '(opposition) number 7' or speaking in long sentences. Anything long or vague either just adds to the background noise or needs some extra information. This sucks the precious time and focus to *provoke* the desired meaning and response by the players. That's right - provoke it.

One of the most dangerous and most prevailing myths about communication is that we can simply 'inject' words into people's minds and they will 'get' them exactly as we meant it. "It's not what our message does to the listener, but what the listener does with our message" is the first, and in my view the most important, of the ten communication laws outlined by social researcher Hugh McKay in his seminal book *Why Don't People Listen*[52]. Goalkeepers' words are there to evoke a response, not shovel information into players' heads. So, goalkeepers just need to say the right things at the right time and all is good, right? Sometimes it is that simple. But there is a lot more to it.

How we say it sometimes matters more than *what* we say. Aggressively threatening or dismissing someone, deservedly or not, may affect them in a way that reduces the chances of them doing their best. Submissively staying quiet and agreeing with someone else while privately disagreeing may eat us away internally for being 'weak' or perhaps deprive the group of a potentially really important insight or contribution we could make.

Circumstances vary, of course, but being assertive in both communication and demeanour probably has the best chance of a goalkeeper provoking the desired meaning in their field players on and off the field. Assertive means expressing your thoughts, feelings and beliefs without undermining yourself or someone else. Being confident, self-assured, honest, direct and making constructive declarations without being aggressive or submissive creates a strong positive presence of a goalkeeper and also raises their levels of self-efficacy, discussed in chapter 5.

Communication is basically sharing of meaning. Because of this we can never separate the message from the relationships in which this sharing takes place. It matters not just what and how it is said but who says it to whom. One of my former teammates noted that he liked how I regularly 'did the thinking for him' and he simply grew to trust my calls. Ever seen a goalkeeper screaming at and gesticulating towards their defenders (I better not look at my own old tapes...)? An inexperienced, usually younger, goalkeeper holding back from saying things too loudly, or at all? What about a goalkeeper and a central defender that know each other so well they barely need to speak during the game to work in perfect unison? All of the above are examples of the relationship and sharing of meaning (or lack of it) at work.

Because of their importance in the team, their largely unobstructed view, the wide lens vision, and the comparatively rested state to the field players, goalkeepers are often afforded the trust to command. They are expected not just to read the game but to be good communicators and help players with their calls. If this relationship and trust between goalkeepers and field players is not present or is perhaps unbalanced, the results can be disastrous. Short term in team conceding goals, long term in affecting the team dynamics. The English goalkeeping legend Peter Shilton put it this way: *"As a goalkeeper you need to be good at organising the people in front of you and motivating them. You need to see what's going on and react to the threats. Just like a good manager in business."*

Communication is also a lot more than speaking well and moving people around. The other, probably as important if not even more important aspect of communication is listening. Listening is an active, meaning making, cognitive process, vastly different from the mere physical process of hearing.

Genuine listening is also risky. It means considering someone else's thoughts with the possibility of us being changed in the process. No, I am not suggesting that goalkeepers should suddenly become super attentive to every one of their field player's inner thoughts and expressions during a game. Nor am I suggesting that just because goalkeepers listen to field players they should proceed to tell them on every occasion what they should do. It can get annoying very quickly. Not convinced? Just imagine the opposite being the case. I don't think there is a self-respecting goalkeeper in the world that wants to be told what they should do in goals all the time by their field players. But listening and trying to understand the players, learning what they do and what is going on for them runs a far greater chance of goalkeepers being good, trusted and intelligent communicators with their teammates. People are simply more likely to listen if we listen to them but also understand there are good and bad times and places for it. This has a direct effect on the next aspect of a goalkeeper's presence - their ability to lead.

Look up 'leadership' and you will have millions of hits on what it is, what types have been identified over the years and which ones are currently in fashion. Various gurus from the airport book stands promote their particular view of leadership and how to develop it, particularly in business settings. In some regards borrowing these insights is useful. After all, leadership is about dealing with human beings and they are no different in business or goalkeeping. However, we do need to be careful in attempting to clone things from one context to another. Any goalkeeper is a part of the particular surroundings in which they live, train and play. Just like their identity, discussed in chapter 2, varies depending on what they bring to their surroundings and what the situation brings to them, so does the way they lead and influence others. Leadership is not a 'thing', it is *always and only* a relation to and with others.

The capacity of goalkeepers to lead and by doing so establish a strong, positive presence depends on several aspects. We have just seen how important good communication is not just in winning games but in the process of developing trust between goalkeepers, their teammates and others in the organisations they are a part of.

The next aspect of leadership is goalkeeper's accountability. Doing your job well and accepting own mistakes is a mark of a leader. Arguments about a conceded goal or lost game can slip, subtly or sometimes very openly, into ugly one or two-way blame game. When we blame, we usually look for *the* culprit, want to punish them and move on. This may placate and satisfy momentarily but it is like a sugar hit and counterproductive in the long run for several reasons. People get defensive because blame gets personal and/or implies the failure was deliberate. Blaming can take the energy away from accepting failure that is often more complex than one person's action or lack of it. Blaming the culprit can also arrest learning from failure and devising solutions to avoid it next again. Sure, consequences against recalcitrance or failure to perform may be well justified sometimes. The final result, a conceded goal or a lost game, may be the same but there is a big difference between a player failing to cover that corner or perhaps a goalkeeper letting in a shot because they couldn't or didn't know how to do it and because they did it out of laziness or even spite.

The idea of 'responsibility' may be a more helpful approach to use here. Identifying and accepting what responsibility one or more players and the goalkeeper had in the failure encourages growth and promotes responsibility. Responsibility says "What went wrong here? What can be done differently?" It is future focused but informed by the past, not stuck in it.

Goalkeepers are no different in this respect. A goalkeeper who is a leader with a great presence will know when to sharply and astutely call to account and when to positively encourage a better effort to learn towards next time from themselves and/or their teammates. The greater the goalkeepers' past experience and maturity the greater their repertoire of suitable responses to draw from to lead effectively. This is not to just blindly repeat 'the old and true' in a new context (new team, club, country, culture ...). Instead, the great leaders pay attention to manoeuvre and manage expectations in dynamic environments when required. A novel way of dealing with a common problem of say conceding late goals or energising defenders may be better than hammering out the same old way but harder. It takes a leader to recognise that. The more goalkeepers are able to use available resources to make judgements in the face of current challenges, the greater the chance of successful leadership. Making the most of what you have in a given situation is what people respect and look up to, whatever the environment.

The best goalkeepers lead by example. They push but also pull their teams along. As for their own aspirations, the clearer and more expansive they are the more likely goalkeepers are to inspire action in others. Or as the proverb says "you can't light a fire with a wet match". There are countless ways to do that.

There is however *one* thing that goalkeepers must *never* do. As someone in the most responsible position on the field, the decider of games and leader by design or by choice - they must never give up, no matter how desperate the situation or surrounds they find themselves in. If at times the field players give up, fellow players and the goalkeeper may cover for some of their shortcomings. There is hope of preventing or perhaps limiting the loss. No such safety net for the goalkeeper! Even when the goals pile on and when the defence is clearly outrun, a goalkeeper giving up and not even trying is a sad sight, more obvious and more deflating than but the most outrageous acts of laziness and incompetence by the field players.

Perhaps the best way to summarise what makes a goalkeeper a good leader is to point out the opposite. An incompetent goalkeeper with poor communication skills, a hypocrite quick to blame others without owning their own mistakes, with limited experience in terms of depth and length, low aspirations, unable or unwilling to make decisions with the given resources and one that gives up easily is not a leader with a strong presence on and off the field for their team.

The above summary does need a word of perspective and caution though. None of this happens in a vacuum so let's not only hold the goalkeeper responsible for what they lack. Some places may *not* be conducive to goalkeepers developing presence through leadership no matter how much they want and try to. Not sure? Think of an environment [53]where goalkeepers are 'second class citizens' and not expected to say much, a group with a habit of blaming each other, a club where a young goalkeeper is 'thrown to the wolves' with no experience, a team with a poor competitive spirit, a squad with players and resources below any acceptable level and more. You will see that for all their best efforts and intentions, developing leadership is a hard if not impossible task for some goalkeepers out there.

So just how then to develop the presence in goalkeepers? Hint - no, it is not all down to their personality. If you work with goalkeepers, please do scratch and dig a little under the surface of things. Presence may appear easy, 'common sense' and could be simply shrugged off as a natural gift or lack of it, like some sort of personality or character trait that doesn't need any work on or compensation for. Just like positioning, diving, catching, blocking and other technical skills of goalkeeping, the presence *can*, and dare say *must* be developed and worked on in a modern goalkeeper.

First of course is the goalkeeper's competence, the foundation of presence. Beware however the assumption that just because skilled goalkeepers, like any elite athletes, make what they do look easy, it actually is easy to do. Competence and the presence it generates is a matter of degrees and takes time.

Achieving, acknowledging and enjoying the growing levels of competence, particularly when newly found, is one of the key things that brings goalkeepers back to face never-ending bruises and attacks after all.

Expecting a beginner to become competent too fast and ignoring instead of validating the budding competence in the search for perfection at the elite level later on really is not helpful. Recognise and enjoy the personal and team wins, big or small, in the challenge of getting better.

Communication skills certainly can be developed, starting from the simplest calls of the shot clock or major patterns of play. As the demand for tactical knowledge increases, it is irresponsible to leave goalkeepers out of drills, conversations and simulations that would make the goalkeeper understand, recognise and then communicate patterns of play to their field players. Tactics are as much as goalkeepers' business as anyone else's. Goalkeepers need to fully understand the game beyond the goalmouth and are expected to speak up effectively. This is not just a matter of 'personality'. It can be practised, but *always* best with the interest of the whole team in mind. A goalkeeper who is a natural chatterbox may have to be curbed to stop the field players getting annoyed with them. Another goalkeeper who is a quiet mouse may need to be awakened to roar if the team needs their calls and encouragement. Becoming a good observer, listener and effective talker (not just a loud or annoying one) complements the presence, builds trust and understanding between the goalkeeper and their team and makes the obstacle for the opposition even more formidable. As for the statement that some goalkeepers are 'natural leaders' - it may be true, but hard work beats talent when talent doesn't work hard enough.

All of these elements help create the seen, felt and seemingly magic intimidation, reassurance and wisdom radiating from the goalkeeper - the presence. The surest way to achieve maximum effect with minimum effort.

'Idol' by Sebastian Lasic

8

Idols and role models

"Guy McKenna."

This was the answer to the question "who is your sporting
idol?" by a 15 years old female on entry into an elite junior
water polo programme at the Western Australian Institute of
Sport (WAIS). You have probably never heard of Guy McKenna[54],
one of the best Aussie Rules Football players in the 1990s. He is a
nice guy and I am sure he was and may still be an idol to many.
What struck me about this answer is that it came shortly after a
monumental event in the very sport these young female athletes
played. Three months earlier, the Australian Womens Water
Polo team won the gold medal at the 2000 Sydney Olympics
in what can only be described as a fairytale. The winning goal
against the USA was scored by a local girl in the last second of
the game at home Olympics in front of the ecstatic and by far the
biggest crowd for any water polo match in history (a record held
until 2016!). This was just the cherry on top of an amazing and

relentless fight these women and their predecessors put up for decades to have women's water polo included in the Olympics. It finally happened, on home soil and for the first time ever. The media and fans could not get enough of them!

But wait ... there's more. Three players of the golden team hailed from and lived in Western Australia and played in the same clubs as these young aspiring juniors. Two field players, one of them the Olympic team captain and at the time arguably the best female water polo player on the planet, and her sister, one of the two goalkeepers on the team. You would be excused to shake your head in disbelief by now thinking could this young girl pick a male footballer rather than a living legend of the very sport she aspires to achieve in and shortly after such a public triumph.

But wait ... she was not the only one either! Only *one* of the eighteen girls in the squad I have just started to coach put the mentioned captain of the golden team as their sporting idol! There were other footballers, basketball players (mostly male too), a hockey player, and a couple of girls' mums who had played water polo at the state and national level. Now, I acknowledge that a proper discussion about idols and role models, gender roles, (lack of) changes in sport as a 'masculine' pursuit[55] could be necessary here but it would fill another book, well beyond the scope of this one. I was however genuinely fascinated and surprised with the girls' responses as I thought the local golden trio or someone similar would top their list of sporting idols. I had a problem on my hand. A problem?

We love to watch and copy people we see as successful. Next time you see kids copy the style, mannerisms, style of play, even the branded gear (serious money anyone?) used by the sports stars you are watching this very thing. Models show us that something we want to do can be done, how to do it well and that in turn helps us achieve it ourselves by trying to copy and/or emulate it. These second-hand or *vicarious experiences* are one of the four sources of self-efficacy, a concept coined by psychologist Albert Bandura mentioned in chapter 5. Self-efficacy is the belief in one's capacity and skill to successfully perform or persist at a particular task in time. Watching others model successfully doing something we want to do increases our self-efficacy, their failure decreases it.

According to the self-efficacy theory, vicarious experiences are particularly powerful if three conditions are met. First is that we consider the person we watch as someone competent. If not, it's easy to dismiss their great performance as a fluke (and that may well be justified). The second condition is that the person we watch is close to the level of our skill. That way we see what they do as something eminently doable by ourselves: "If (s)he can do it, so can I!" Thirdly, watching others is particularly powerful when we have much to learn and we are keen to do so.

Given this you could probably understand why I considered my athletes' responses as a problem. Why would these aspiring youngsters *not* idolise the supremely skilled local legends that were just like them only a few years ago and who they could literally see down at the pool several times a week. Or maybe they did but they weren't their 'idols'? Was the language of the question the reason for the surprise results? Probably. Both.

Let's make some important distinctions between 'idols' and 'role models' as understood in this book. They all certainly share the characteristic of being a model of someone who we see as better than ourselves but they are not necessarily the same thing. NBA legend Charles Barkley caused a stir in 1993 with his Nike commercial[56] stating "I'm not a role model. I am not paid to be one. Just because I dunk a basketball doesn't mean I should raise your kids." I am not entering the polemic here and you can search the clip and responses to it yourself. I do however recall Barkley chuckling many years later that he must be "the only guy in the history of the world to get criticised for telling kids to listen to their parents as the preferred role models." So let's clear up the language here but with a caveat that this is not a definitive but just one possible delineation of the two terms.

Imagine a continuum. On one side, there are idols.[57] They are the infallible, god-like, almost untouchable persons in terms of access to and possibly achievement. They are 'the best', even 'perfect', no matter how irrational and unsupported by various data this claim may be. Idols are often heavily mediated, produced through mainstream and/or social media. They are real persons of course but it's a largely one-way relationship with us. We hardly personally interact, apart from perhaps brief, chance encounters via social media or in person, but we mostly admire them or even fawn in their presence. Our idols may have their darker sides but we ignore or minimise these because we want to bask in the glow they project. We admire them for what we see they do, most of it on the sporting field. If famous and able to, we buy their posters, gear they endorse, watch their games ... you get the picture, I am sure.

On the other side of the continuum are role models. Literally, a model of what we would like to look, sound, be like in the role we are in now or one realistically achievable in the future. They are admired but they may be more accessible to us. The relationship is more likely to be a two-way one as we may even know them personally and interact with them. In this we are more likely to see and acknowledge the multiple sides of the same person. We don't (just) blindly see perfection, we see and accept the lot. We look up to them not just for what they do but who they are on as well as off the sporting field.

In most cases the reality is probably somewhere between these two ends as people we look up to carry elements of being both an idol and a role model[58]. So why separate them? Simply because having both may be useful. It is like having dreams on one side and goals on the other. This is something touched on in chapter 5 but deserves a reminder. Dreams, like idols, often lie in the (far) future, may not be realistic and hardly in our control but unless we 'shoot for the stars' we may never even consider, let alone reach the level of our sporting idols. This is why I am very happy for our son to be an avid follower of Jan Oblak, a maestro in goals for Atletico Madrid and Slovenia and regularly considered one of the very best football goalkeepers in the world. He watches the clips of Jan, trains in a green goalie top with Oblak emblazoned on the back of it and sometimes pretends that he is playing, like his idol, a great game in front of thousands of adoring fans. It is a healthy fantasy but a fantasy nonetheless. And while he might try to pretend and copy Oblak's moves, he knows they are way above his level of skill and that's OK. We are certainly not banking our family's fortune on our youngest replacing Oblak in goals at Atletico.

Goals, like the role models on our little continuum, are much more close, personal and reachable aspirations. This is where the role models do their work - in the seemingly small, daily choices, from technical details to general attitude. To move effectively in goals. To bravely face shots. To anticipate play. To communicate well. To not skip that training session when you may not feel like going. To look out for a teammate when down. To get up for that second, third effort when needed. To always be on time and ready for training. To deal with disappointment in a good way. To learn and want to get better. To stay after training and practice that one thing just a little more. Endless list really, but of completely *doable* things that one can see a role model do. To each of these examples above, add the words 'like I really could...' and you have powerful role modelling at work, and one that can work in both desirable or undesirable ways. Pick a bad role model and you will soon see the effects of it too.

A healthy merger of fantasy and realistic aspiration can be a wonderful thing but like many other things about goalkeeping described in this book - it's no magic. It takes time and effort to create an environment where both fantasy and realistic aspiration flourish. A place where the nurture we provide for goalkeepers stimulates and supports their natural ability and interest. Such 'living and breathing' of sport and goalkeeping is much easier, much richer and arguably much less taxing in the surroundings where idols and good role models abound. But even in surrounds where everything seems to be ideal, success is not assured. The danger lies in assuming that just because we provide the best nurture in terms of coaching, support and role models, the natural ability and interest for goalkeeping should be there by default. Good nurture does not guarantee success, it only increases the chances of it. Soberingly, the world is full of promising ex-junior stars who gave up not just goalkeeping but sport altogether fed up with the unmet expectations, sometimes in environments where it looked like everything was provided for them and all they had to was to … succeed.

On the other side, there have been thousands of successful goalkeepers who have turned up to training and work largely on their own. For them, the (more remote) idols and role models from different aspects of sport and life have provided the main source of vicarious experiences, guidance and inspiration. I had some wonderful role models as a youngster but I honestly wish I had YouTube and the internet growing up as a goalkeeper too. There have been and will continue to be many goalkeeping trailblazers overcoming tremendous odds to succeed. Natural ability of course can and does sometimes flourish despite the relative lack of nurture. But things may be very hard if all we have is ourselves, without someone to guide, to share, to learn from, listen and to look up to as a goalkeeper.

The daily reality for most goalkeepers is, again, somewhere between these two positions. That's OK but whatever the mix of natural ability and nurturing environment it is a good idea to have idols and, especially, good role models. Apart from direct modelling of technique, performance or attitude, there is another reason for it that many goalkeepers will recognise next.

In chapter 6 I acknowledged the physical and particularly mental challenge of goalkeepers vying for that single, hard-to-dislodge spot in goals with their daily training partners. Yes, we learn by watching each other but we also compare with each other and the fewer empirical markers to separate us the more subjective the comparison becomes. Two runners or swimmers may have their best race times to ultimately decide who makes the team. Selecting a goalkeeper is a much more complex affair, an issue expanded upon in chapter 10. Training partners are a constantly visible yardstick of goalkeeping to each other. We consciously and subconsciously make judgements about who does what better.

What may sometimes start as a healthy competition and perhaps mutual admiration between training partners can quickly turn the other way towards envy and/or a spot of *schaden-freude* when our training partner *and* opponent for the spot fails at something. Seeing someone similar to us fail may decrease our self-efficacy but hey, "it increases my selection chances, I just have to be better than the other goalkeeper." This begs the question - are our 'opponents' within the same team good role models to have?

No and yes. 'No' when the only aim is to beat our opponent. This may sound a little counterintuitive because it goes against winning as the essence of sport. But what if our training partner and goalkeeping opponent we watch and compare ourselves against is not really that great in the first place? Instead of being content by beating them we could do better to look up to someone better than that. Similarly, we may start focusing too much on what *they* do and which is out of our control, rather than focusing on our *own* improvement that largely *is* in our control. Constant comparison with our training partner can be very taxing and can generate unhelpful levels of anxiety.

'Yes' when the roles of opponent and role model merge into one. Imagine a young goalkeeper starting to work with an older and respected goalkeeper and pushing for their spot, trying to emulate them. Competing against the person they hold up to be a role model is an acknowledgement for both. It is a marker of achievement for the young or less experienced to have reached the stage and can perhaps go beyond. It is also a mark of worth for the older goalkeeper to have served as a role model. Expect the role model to fight as any champion would, but it becomes a matter of mutual respect to push each other.

In both cases above, the process may look the same but the underlying motivation is very different. In the first instance, we end up looking *at*, even *down* on our training partner to feel better. In the second case, we are looking *up to* someone better than ourselves and, very likely, earn their respect by reaching that level. Lesson in all this?

Instead of comparing yourself against some remote idol you may never emulate or just the person you have to beat to make the cut, find and compare yourself against the very best goalkeepers you can realistically see, reach and become one yourself. This may free you up from the sometimes daily anxiety of comparing yourself with a direct goalkeeping 'opponent' and/or laziness should they turn out to be worse than you. Chances are it will earn you two things better and faster too - that spot on the team and respect. Some would see seeking someone better than themselves as an admittance of their incompetence, even humiliation. Definitely not a mark of a champion in goalkeeping, sport or beyond! Or as Sir Arthur Conan Doyle would say through the mouth of Sherlock Holmes: "Mediocrity knows nothing higher than itself; but talent instantly recognises genius."

Importantly, having a role model is not about being someone's clone. Copying someone may be an act of learning, acknowledgement, even flattery, but ultimately - we are all different. Yes, there are universal laws of physics but we all have our own ways of moving our bodies to follow them. Yes, we may call them the same but we also have our own combinations and patterns of feeling, thinking, learning. We may and do pick up things from others but ultimately it is what we reject, incorporate or tweak as a whole person with our own histories and our own physical and mental abilities that creates the beautiful diversity of goalkeeping. This diversity is also the strength of goalkeeping, not an impediment to some sort of perfection, measurable or imagined, to be cloned.

And just what makes a good role model? How to be one? The answers are as diverse as we are so I am reluctant to moralise on the 'good' here. Instead, I prefer to call it an 'impactful' or perhaps 'influential' role model. Whatever the motivation, it may be a good idea to consider two things as a role model.

First is the awareness of your own values. What is it that you project, what are you an example of? For a balanced view, check that with both your admirers and your detractors as well as, importantly, yourself. People do and will see who is comfortable in their skin and who is not. I dare say the former have a much greater chance of being an impactful role model than the latter.

Secondly, being a role model is *not* our choice to make. This was one of the key criticisms of the mentioned attempt by Charles Barkley to free athletes from what can be a burden of role modelling. Whether we aspire to be a role model one or shy away from it, we can't force people to look up to us or look away from us as one. In other words, the moment you are in the public eye there is a chance you are or will be a role model to someone. Get used to the fact that while you may be, suspect or even expect to be a role model, you may very rarely know the full extent of it too.

And if you are looking for a suitable role model - how do you find one? Again, stating some universal truths of 'suitability' here would be almost disrespectful considering the diversity of views, needs and contexts. One possible direction I can propose is to consider 'the head and the heart'. The head will ask questions like: Do I like what I see (in this goalkeeper, person…)? Do we share similar values? What is it that I like about them? Is that better than what I do? Can I realistically do and be like that now or or perhaps in the future? If the honest answers by the head match what the heart likes - you have got yourself a suitable role model.

Back to my 'problem' of the young female water polo players idolising a football guy I started with. Still see it as a problem?

As far as having idols and role models from your own sport being better from a technical perspective and being a part of the culture of your sport - yes, it was a problem. We worked on it and gradually built a culture where the girls increasingly looked for those reinforcing vicarious experiences and role models within their own sport. However, I never discouraged any of them to look beyond that for athletes to look up to. After all, one of the founding ideas behind this book was for goalkeepers to raise their heads and look to their brothers and sisters in different sports to learn, sustain and inspire.

I invite you to do exactly that!

'That's It!' by Sebastian Lasic

9

Teaching and learning the craft

"How do you teach a goalkeeper? The way they learn best."

This may sound like a simple and self-evident truism but there is a lot more to it. So far in this book, we have explored many things to do with bringing up a goalkeeper or growing up as one. Truth is, no one was born a goalkeeper so everything we know about goalkeeping is … learned. But 'learning' is another one of those commonly used words that becomes slippery when we start looking at it closely.

Before starting my work in education and coaching almost three decades ago, I used to see learning merely as a natural process, like breathing. Something we do all the time, can't stop it until we die. My view on learning has evolved since. Sure, our brain synapses and with it memories form, strengthen, weaken and die constantly but learning is so much more than that. If we assume that is *all* that learning is, we are dismissing the relationships between the learner and what they learn (content), why they learn (purpose) and who they learn from as irrelevant. In other words, "it doesn't matter what goalkeepers learn, why they learn it and who they learn it with or from, as long as they learn." Really? I trust you see the ridiculousness of that statement.

Dutch education scholar Gert Biesta put it well when he said that when we refer to something as 'learning', "we are not describing a naturally occurring phenomenon but are actually making a judgement about change."[59]

We also don't just learn for the sake of learning that goes on in our head and nobody can see. We want to put what we learned to some use, test or display. We ... perform! Performance inevitably generates judgement. Because of this judgement, we prefer to look good to ourselves and others.

I used to see learning and performance as two different things. I would say to my high school students "performance is about doing and not screwing up, learning is about screwing up and doing it better next time." I used this neat, nice sounding distinction while working with hundreds of disengaged teenagers in some pretty tough schools. It helped establish a 'failure-positive' environment in which they were encouraged to give an honest try in learning something I wanted them to learn but without worrying about the performance and being judged, usually poorly so. Many of those students had very low levels of self-efficacy and their disengagement was a defence mechanism. It was a way to avoid negative judgement they have had plenty of in their past. Giving them the space to learn from both their mistakes and the little wins they had was a good way to raise their self-efficacy and re-engage. Many of them did just that!

But despite the successes with these students, I gradually realised that the 'performance versus learning' dichotomy can be a false one. It begged a further question: When do we then seek to encourage and when to eliminate mistakes?

The legendary cartoonist Randy Glasbergen[60] explained this conundrum best.

"If we learn from our mistakes, shouldn't
I try to make as many mistakes as possible?"

Image used with permission by the author

I have acknowledged several times in this book how responsible the role of a goalkeeper is in any team and how very costly their mistakes can be. Surely then we wouldn't encourage goalkeepers making mistakes and instead focus on success, right? Well, mistakes and successes are actually the same thing - feedback. But whether we see feedback as positive ('success') or negative ('mistake') and the magnitude of it depends on the lenses we look through.

One of these lenses is the perceived level of importance. The higher the stakes, the more important the performance and 'making sure you don't screw up' becomes. This of course depends on the expectations of each individual, their team, family, club, even entire country, and the cost of failure, personal and/or shared. Sometimes the level of expectations and with it importance matches in a healthy way. For example, every player in the team recognises how important the game is so they prepare for it together, a coach figures out their goalkeeper doesn't need the extra pressure so they give them space to prepare in peace, parents acknowledge that despite all the support they have provided their child may simply not be as interested in becoming the next big thing as they are hoped for so they relax and enjoy watching them just play with friends...the list is endless.

Equally endless is the list of mismatches of perceived importance, from high-level doping cheats to weekend junior games. Ever seen the 'ugly parents' at junior sport and their either embarrassed, fearful or perhaps narcissistic and overly precocious offspring? Our own football club prides itself on the sense of perspective and has signs like these put up around junior pitches for a good reason.

PLEASE REMEMBER
These are kids.
This is a game.
The coaches are volunteers.
The referee s are human.
This is NOT the FIFA World Cup.
MELVILLE CITY FC
www.melvillecityfc.com.au

We also see and interpret mistakes through the lens of perceived competence. The model of four levels of competence[61] is a common and useful way of looking at this concept. At the level of 'unconscious incompetence', goalkeepers make mistakes without understanding or knowing how to do something. Complete beginners don't necessarily recognise what they lack. They don't know what they don't know or they perhaps even deny or argue that a particular skill we try to teach them is or will be useful to them. With circumstances, strong enough drive or perhaps an incentive to recognise their incompetence, goalkeepers get to the next stage of 'conscious incompetence'. Here they don't understand or know how to do something (yet...) but they realise the value of a (new) skill so they invest in learning. At this stage, making mistakes is absolutely *crucial* and should not be discouraged. More than making them, *learning from* mistakes that still may regularly occur is encouraged. The joy comes not so much from being perfect but from the feeling of making progress. Next is the level of 'conscious competence'. At this level, goalkeepers understand or know how to do something but it requires a great deal of deliberate thought and concentration. Skills may be broken down into steps, and there is a heavy conscious involvement in their execution. Some mistakes still occur but successful executions of various skills are more common and increasingly expected. Eventually, goalkeepers have practised skills so much that they become 'second nature' and can be performed easily in a state of 'unconscious competence'. This frees the resources to attend to other tasks. Levels of expected performance rise and mistakes stand out because they are either very rare and/or very costly. The enjoyment comes from perfection, often achieved too.

If the *perceptions* of competence match the *expectations* of competence, it is more likely that goalkeepers will be a lot more comfortable in seeing mistakes as something to accept early on but gradually, and rightfully so, minimise as their competence grows. Realities of course can be very different. In their well-meaning and excitement, coaches, parents, other (in)vested parties and goalkeepers themselves sometimes overestimate their level of competence. In the rush to realise the goalkeeper's perceived ability and potential as soon as possible and as best as possible, they seek to minimise mistakes and 'screwing up'. However, making mistakes is an integral part of the learning process. Trying to somehow eliminate them too early, too often or too intensely deprives the goalkeeper of the important feedback *they* need and use to process, learn and develop. We can give a goalkeeper all the tips and drills in the world but we can't learn and develop *for* them.

Adequately supported goalkeepers become more resilient if they have had a chance to make, learn from and overcome mistakes in the past, especially as they become more costly. Even at the highest level of competence there will of course be some unintended mistakes to learn from. But an elite coach or elite athlete dismissing or trying to positively spin a shockingly poor game by prattling on about how "what they learned from that game is more important than winning" is not a good sight. That sentiment is essential in working with the 'incompetent' juniors but laughable with pros, paid for their 'unconscious competence'.

Importantly, just like goalkeepers, coaches also undergo this process of increased competence. As it happens, many goalkeeping coaches are current or ex goalkeepers themselves and bring with them a certain level of competence to start with. This begs a question: Are goalkeepers, current or ex, better than non-goalkeepers in working with goalkeepers? After all, as the football goalkeeping legend Gianluigi Buffon stated *"the role of a goalkeeper is difficult to judge, above all if you haven't been a goalkeeper. It's like me giving an opinion on someone's job without having had any experience in their sector. You start to realise how many stupid things are said and written about goalkeepers."* Often very true. I hope this book is not one of those stupid things...

Specialist knowledge is of course an asset in working with goalkeepers. Sound knowledge and deep(er) understanding of the value and intricacies of goalkeeping creates a larger repertoire to draw upon in working with them. Personal experience as a goalkeeper adds another valuable dimension to it, even if from another sport (someone should write a book about that...). However, personal experience is much more effective as a tool for *reflection* rather than validation. Using your own, unique goalkeeping experience to reflect on similarities and differences between your experiences and those of who you work with is great. It helps goalkeepers you work with to get comfortable in *their* own skin. But if using your goalkeeping experience in coaching goalkeepers to validate your ego, vicariously relive some past personal glory, create someone a carbon copy of yourself, preach exclusively what has worked for you instead of humbly asking 'what could work for this goalkeeper' - your goalkeeping experience might actually be a hindrance. This could be despite the undoubtedly best intentions and the passion you bring to it.

A degree of humility, openness to learning, resourcefulness in getting good advice and role models can and do overcome the lack of coach's personal experience in goals. Give me a non-goalkeeper with those qualities to work with goalkeepers any time over an ex-goalkeeper with experience in goals but without the curiosity and humility to recognise constant changes in the game and the possible limitations of their own ways of goalkeeping!

Specialist goalkeeping knowledge can also be wasted in many ways. We may pitch our advice at the wrong 'level of competence' and importance; we may be unable to convert deep and what Polanyi called 'tacit knowledge'[62] into explicit, understandable instruction and/or feedback; assume goalkeeper's ability and prior knowledge without bothering to check or break down the steps; have a poor relationship with with the goalkeeper we are working with, and more. Knowing goalkeeping and things about it is great but without 'knowing the audience' and knowing how to relate and communicate with goalkeepers, much of what an expert says will either be lost, ignored at best, or lead to confusion, even a sense of inadequacy at worst!

Fortunately, and by the nature of their position that forces them to be so, (good) goalkeepers are often also great students of the game themselves. In this process, there are definitely times for telling goalkeepers what to do. But there are also times to encourage and, ultimately, empower goalkeepers to study, learn about the game and themselves. The process starts with asking them questions like these below. This is far from an exhaustive list and I am sure you would adjust the language and type of questions but I trust you get the idea.

- What did you learn (from the game, training, tournament...)?
- What do you think you did well? What can improve on?
- What would you like to see/have seen happen in that session/game/tournament?
- Which of these things are you in control of?
- What are your options? ...

Importantly, for such questions to really have an impact and encourage goalkeeper's own thinking, the coach would ask them with *genuine* curiosity, not as a fake way of generating answers they want to hear. Just as important as asking is *listening* well to the goalkeeper's answers. Listening is a cognitive and emotional act, very different from the mere physical process of hearing. Good listening means opening your mind and heart to the person in front of you, regardless of the difference in your age, experience and knowledge. Sounds nice but don't be fooled - this sort of listening is hard, almost unnatural for some of us coaches. Firstly because in our daily lives we tend to mostly use conversational listening that is quick, informal and less cognitively taxing. Secondly, deep listening can be hard because of a possible attitude that "a coach is there to tell not to listen." With such an underlying attitude, we are less likely to open our mind and instead listen only for the confirmation of our own thoughts, ideas and solutions.

As difficult as it may be, listening (more) deeply is well worth the effort. Listening to beginners, still largely incompetent, builds relationships and gives us a better chance of giving advice that is not only correct but appropriate for their level of development and understanding. Listening deeply to an emerging or already competent goalkeeper is a stepping stone to the next level - empowerment.

This means encouraging the goalkeeper's curiosity and giving *them* the authority (and with it *responsibility!*) to figure some things out for themselves. The crucial aspect here is holding back the instinct to tell and advise goalkeepers and stifle *their* thinking, *their* solutions, no matter how 'right' we may be. No, this does *not* mean we just best leave the goalkeepers to figure it all out by themselves. Absolutely not! In a partnership, the coaches' job changes from mostly telling to (also) sharing their own thoughts to *stimulate* goalkeeper's own, perhaps steering goalkeepers away from utterly wasteful or potentially dangerous ideas, and getting them to justify, commit and be *accountable* for the proposed solutions. These could include having input in the design of training based on what they need, what they want to work on or perhaps try, ways of coping with anxiety, ways of analysing the opposition, a change in a tactical or technical aspect of some kind ... another endless list.

There is a good chance the shared solutions driven by the goalkeeper, particularly if more mature and experienced, will be identical or at least similar, perhaps even better to what the coach had in mind. However, there will be one massive difference - the goalkeeper will *own* the solutions and because of that care *a lot more* about them than if they were spoonfed by the coach. Yes, some goalkeepers and coaches may not like this because it may well mean extra work for them. But in the long run, this approach expands knowledge, builds initiative, relationships, accountability and ends up producing a(nother) smart goalkeeper ready to work with the next generation.

This again is not an easy thing to do. Sports coaches enjoy being helpful to their athletes and being 'right'. Many are paid to be exactly that and appreciate the simple(r), army-like, hierarchical flow of power and knowledge (French philosopher Michel Foucault[63] gave us all a fascinating theory on this). As such they are often looked up to provide the 'right' answer(s) by athletes. That's OK and sometimes very necessary at any level. But a goalkeeper thinking about, generating, critically justifying and owning their solutions is possibly more valuable than a mountain of expert knowledge the coach is busting to throw at the goalkeeper.

What if the coach is *not* an expert on goalkeepers but has to work with them? Even more reasons to listen to and empower the goalkeepers! Collaboration, learning in coming up with the solutions with goalkeepers is a great chance to grow together. The hardest aspect in such situations can be the humility to 'level' and learn together rather than the lack of specialist goalkeeper knowledge to 'pass on'. Again, and I can't stress this more, empowering goalkeepers does *not* mean rubbing hands off responsibility for goalkeepers' training and development, leaving them to their own devices and just blaming them if/when they don't learn or perform well. That is coaching incompetence at best and cowardice at worst.

So is there an ideal way to bring up a goalkeeper? It is a question we can never know the exact and universal answer to due to the complexities of each goalkeeper and the environments they are brought up in. Some approaches may validate what you do, others won't. That's OK, but I do invite you to honestly reflect on your strengths and weaknesses in providing what the goalkeeper in front of you needs. You may not have a library of goalkeeping drills in your head but you may be a great listener, motivator, learner ... If you do your best with what you have, your conscience is clear no matter what you do.

Perhaps a better question than 'what is the best way' would be 'what matters?' in teaching goalkeepers and learning to be one? I dip into the field of education again and this time borrow my good friend's Dr Deborah Netolicky list[64], adjusted here for the sports and goalkeeping context.

Goalkeepers matter. Both 'goalkeepers' in plural as part of the ongoing, rich story within and across different sports as well as each and every individual goalkeeper with all their idiosyncrasies, circumstances, attitudes, dreams and abilities. A coach is there for the goalkeeper, not the other way around.

Coaches matter. While goalkeeper's attitudes and available resources are arguably bigger influences, coaches are the biggest on-site factor in making a difference to goalkeeper development.

Knowledge matters. Not information but knowledge. The stuff we learn not from experience but from reflecting on experience. The stuff we process, make sense of and with the help of effective stimulus create and store in our long term memory (in the case of motor skills in our 'small brain', see chapter 4). Once there, it leaves us with the space and the fluency to focus on the finer details at hand. Critical thinking needs knowledge on which to build, creativity works best by knowing the foundations on which to innovate.

Coaching matters. Don't just leave goalkeepers on their own. Then as coaches working with them or perhaps goalkeepers themselves, we can never stop asking critical questions like:

- How do I/we decide what to do (with that goalkeeper or a group of them)?
- On what evidence do I/we base our decisions?
- How do I/we know that is in the best interests of the goalkeeper and the team?

If we want goalkeepers to learn, *they* need to be the ones who are doing the thinking and the doing *to learn* (remember Biesta's claim learning is not a process but a judgement about the rate of change). We can show, advise, suggest, invite, stimulate and many other things but we can never learn and progress *for* them. Ever!

Relationships matter. We may not even be aware of it but we see everything and everyone we interact with in relation to ourselves. Relationships and how we affect each other's thoughts and feelings are at the heart of teaching and learning anything because they grease the wheels of any communication between people.

Identity and belonging matters. As mentioned in chapter 2, there is a big difference between 'playing in goals' and 'being a goalkeeper'. The former is doing, the latter is being. How can you put that 'being' in the service of the team?

Environment matters. As pointed out in chapter 8, development and success of a goalkeeper is not all down to their individual skill and drive. Goalkeepers are far more able to thrive in an environment where their role, its uniqueness but also its function as part of the team is acknowledged and supported. A goalkeeper feeling challenged but supported, safe and what psychologists might describe as 'being held' by someone in a high-risk environment of sport and goalkeeping is a wonderful thing. Goalkeepers - who's got your back?

Purpose matters. According to the self determination theory[65] of Deci and Ryan and later adapted and popularised by Dan Pink[66], humans are best motivated by three things in their work once their basic needs are met. A sense of 'autonomy' and self-direction, the urge to get better at something or 'mastery', and the desire to do something that has meaning and is important, or 'purpose', especially when beyond the purely individual sphere.

To me, the last one is particularly important. Humanity's greatest achievements (and atrocities!) have been achieved doing things *for* someone or something other than self. Doing that, things are not necessarily easier to do but are easier to bear and sweeter to celebrate.

Yes, all these things matter. But is there one that matters most, that we should have in mind all the time when goalkeeping or working with goalkeepers? I answer the question with a passage by Mark Upton. He wrote it in the context of applying a particular coaching methodology but when I first read it the words rang so true and so widely applicable in other contexts that they deserve to be reproduced in full:

*"If you had to prioritise one characteristic required of a coach and others involved in player development, **patience** would surely rate a mention. I've already covered the nonlinear nature of learning – sometimes quick, other times slower. This will be the case regardless of the pedagogy employed. I often get the impression people expect to see immediate results after using one approach for one session. If only! Learning Objectives for a session don't help matters, creating the illusion (and unnecessary expectation) that the rate of learning can be fully controlled. The skill of the coach/learning designer is understanding why and how to manipulate constraints when they perceive the developmental progress of a player(s) has stalled for a significant period of time. Identifying the 'rate limiter' is key – this could be technical-tactical, psycho-social or maturation issues. Often life events off the pitch will need attention, highlighting the importance of having good relationships with players and understanding them as people in order to be an effective facilitator of learning."*[67]

Learning. We started the chapter with it. There is no performance, or 'doing' without it. But a goalkeeper who doesn't 'just do their job', as appreciated and essential as this is, but can also reflect, understand, explain, critique and develop what they do is a gift. A gift to themselves and any others they may work with in the future no matter where they go.

Patiently so, of course.

'This One' by Sebastian Lasic

10

Finding and selecting a goalkeeper

"I know what I want. I want to be a soccer goalkeeper."

Toby had been playing indoor five-a-side football with his school friends. Every Friday night, we would go down to the local sports centre and cheer on, laugh and wipe the odd tear with the mighty Purple Penguins as their team was called. The game had a goalkeeper but the kids regularly rotated without much planning, someone always stood in the small goals. There was no formal team training between games, just free kickabouts with family and friends in our backyards and local fields. During one such kickabout at a proper football field with adult goals, Toby stood in goals and enthusiastically, and rather theatrically, made a save after diving save. That day, pictured, he uttered the words above. I knew he was serious.

"How did you become a goalkeeper?" In my conversation for this book and well before, I very rarely came across a goalkeeper that started playing their sport just to be a goalkeeper. Not fit enough to run; could not be bothered to move; tallest; slowest; longest arms; bit lazy; thought it would be fun; didn't like the contact; can't exactly remember; no one else would go in goals; substitute turned out fun; family member was one; coach just put me there; no good in the field; liked the colours; luck of the draw; rotated positions and landed on it … and then began to like something about it, work on it, got better at it. The positive spiral was created and countless goalkeeping careers, some of them short and some amazingly long or decorated began. But most of them started as 'happy accidents'. There are good reasons for that.

We fell in love. We didn't plan it. We found goalkeeping as much as it found us. The level of randomness differs in each case of course. Some have had a greater chance of becoming a goalkeeper than others. No matter what though there had to be a degree of 'right place at the right time' about becoming a goalkeeper to allow the love to begin and flourish in the right mix of internal and external conditions.

The late Dr Vlaho Orlić was a revered mentor of several Olympic and world gold medal winning water polo coaches and players. His methods and wisdom transcended sport in former Yugoslavia and beyond. When he learned I would be coaching young juniors, he asked me: "So, what is your most important job as their coach?" I started talking about the basics of technique, positioning, game sense and so on. What he said next stayed with me for the next three decades of coaching and teaching I have done since. He gently cut me off mid sentence and said:"Tomaž, your most important job is to get these kids to fall in love with the game. Everything else is a lot easier after that." And inside this love for the game, for some of us there is the special call of the goalmouth to answer.

Just how do we then encourage such 'happy accidents' of trying and falling in love with the game and more specifically goalkeeping? Well, we generally like to make ourselves attractive in search of love don't we?

People in different sport settings have done some wonderful things to make goalkeeping attractive, especially in younger categories. They have regularly rotated every player in goals so everyone got a taste of playing in goals not just once but several times at different stages during the season; counted goalkeeper saves as part of the overall score in practice games; provided nice and perhaps little special gear for goalkeepers to wear;

gave goalkeepers a 'job to do' (shout out shot clock times, count passes, spot and encourage teammates' good play) if the game held little action for the sometimes frozen and lonely goalkeeper; got teammates to gather round the goalkeeper at different points of the game (check out how the ice hockey players do it at all levels); gave a separate area to train in; invited experienced goal-keepers for talks, clinics, work as mentors to young goalkeepers; ran awards for goalkeeping; made sure they deliberately noted positive goalkeeper efforts and in many other ways, big and small, made an effort to make goalkeepers feel valued and part of a team, and more. Most importantly, they provided attention to goalkeepers with a human touch and connection, especially when it came in the form of a person working with them and looking after them.

Does it all have to be wonderful to encourage kids to take up goalkeeping? No, it doesn't have to be all sugar and spice. Sometimes the greater the adversity, the greater the love and with it determination to grow, improve and do well as a goalkeeper. Arguably the intrinsic, internal drive and desire to become a good goalkeeper is far more important than any of the extrinsic things we put in place to encourage it. But it is a helluva lot easier to fall in love with goalkeeping and become a good goalkeeper where there is an abundance of incentives, support and good role models.

When it comes to finding and encouraging (young) goalkeepers, one of the most common questions is "what do I look for (in searching for a goalkeeper)?" A very valid question indeed. One thing that can't be ignored are of course physical predispositions like height (current and/or potential), reach, agility and speed. In checking these we do have to keep in mind though that some genetic advantages may show earlier than others. This is especially important to consider before and during puberty as our bodies undergo significant and in some cases quite dramatic changes. For example, the agility of a promising pre-pubescent goalkeeper may be on hold for a year or two (or more!) into puberty as they 'grow into' their adult body. Again, vision, patience and 'playing the long game' can pay big dividends here.

Then there is the perhaps even trickier psychological makeup of a goalkeeper we are looking for. As outlined in chapter 6, looking for an 'ideal' personality type is fraught with danger, especially if framed as 'positive' or 'negative'. We are all different! It is very easy and tempting to go by a template of a goalkeeper we like or perhaps what worked for us as goalkeepers. It is harder but arguably much better to figure out the profile of each goalkeeper and what makes them tick by asking questions like: What is their attitude and how, when does it change? What are the emotions they show and how do they affect them? How do they handle expectations and pressure? Answers to questions like these may provide a decent picture of a (future) goalkeeper.

This picture will of course always be seen through the inescapable lens of our values and expectations of what we are looking for. While views among coaches, goalkeepers and others may differ (not a bad thing per se!), a goalkeeper who can: easily summon and hold intense focus; is not afraid in physical and psychological sense; has satisfactory levels of self-efficacy and 'coachability' to receive feedback and constructive criticism; shows willingness to improve; and emits even at an early age the signs of 'presence' in goals, is the sort of goalkeeper that may be hard to 'produce' but fairly easy to spot if we know what we are looking for.

As for the arguments at what age one should look for and specialise in goalkeeping and how much of it should we do, the best indicator might be the goalkeepers themselves. We may need to keep a madly keen youngster who wants to know every-thing about goalkeeping by the age of ten happy and learning. Admirable and sweet to work with but careful they don't end up as disappointed 'early peakers' a few years later when the peers catch up. The world is full of them. On the other side, we may have to patiently 'hold the space' for a junior that we see as a 'natural goalkeeper' but for whom we have the faith they may develop slightly later. Yes, it is important to lay down those neural paths spoken about in chapters 4 and 9 early so they are there when the body matures. But the early work may be pretty much wasted if the kid does not want to be a goalkeeper later on. I presume wanting to be a 'good' goalkeeper here because being a bad one is not fun for the vast majority of those who try.

Once we find and start to work with a goalkeeper, chances are we will need to evaluate them and possibly decide between two or more goalkeepers which one gets the coveted spot in the squad or team and who misses out. First of all, if you have never coached and made such decisions please know that they are not fun to make. It can be like deciding which of your close friends or workmates you have spent a lot of time together with gets the promotion, or worse. Not always but it can be. This is one of the hardest parts of a coaching job, even when and no matter how much we are paid for it. Yes, coaches are people too.

Different views, aspirations, agendas, egos and (usually) over-expectations that don't match the realities and needs of the team have caused an enormous amount of headaches for coaches when selecting goalkeepers in any sport. In what ways do coaches make that selection call and sleep well at night?

Over the last few decades, the increasing ease of collection and the corresponding rise in the volume of all sorts of data has fuelled the primacy of 'hard', measurable evidence and in making selection decisions. This is done in good faith, mostly to minimise the risk of making poor decisions, and make or perhaps justify decisions with some sort of objective metric (Key Performance Indicators anyone?). The extensive use of measurable, quantified indicators has also changed the way the process of training and performance is monitored and made accountable remotely, by people like funding bodies or sponsors who are not directly involved in the day-to-day operations. Lengthy expansion on this fascinating trend and its well-discussed origins, paths and effects by sociologists, philosophers and others is again beyond the scope of this chapter and book. I mention it here merely to frame the discussion but I invite you to explore the ideas of 'audit society' and performativity further.

Data. Numbers. 'Hard' evidence. 'Numbers don't lie'. 'Clean cut'. As mentioned in chapter 4, there are goalkeepers with higher percentages of saves than others. Drill into the numbers further and they may have a higher percentage of saves against a particular opponent, from a certain shooting zone, when using a particular type of zone defence, higher percentage of successful outlet passes ... There are goalkeepers that verifiably leap, sprint or do something else faster than others, lift more on leg press machine, have lower skinfolds ... another endless list. With new data collection and analytical tools, more sophisticated algorithms, even machine learning and artificial intelligence in use or just on the horizon, we could dashboard the hell out of each goalkeeper and empirically 'prove' that one goalkeeper is better than another (remember 'Moneyball'[68] and baseball sabermetrics?). What is more, we are increasingly expected, and in turn expect, to have decisions legitimised with some sort of metric, calculations and figures. Even some figures are better than no figures, right? We find out what's important, find ways to measure it and then let the numbers do the talking. In this scenario, picking a goalkeeper would be like qualifying the fastest 100m runner - a 'hard', clinical, bias-free, quantifiable evidence-based objective judgement.

Now, applied statistics can be immensely useful, from picking sports teams to fighting global pandemics and planetary climate change. Similarly, setting measurable standards and making sure people do the job they are responsible for according to those standards arguably keeps athletes training well as much as it keeps planes flying safely. But there is a problem, and a guy called William Bruce Cameron (no, not the popularly mis-attributed Albert Einstein) nailed it by stating: "Not everything that can be counted counts, and not everything that counts can be counted."

My biggest career disappointment, a last minute non-selection to the Olympic team, was justified with the words "Peter [the other goalkeeper, not his real name, nice guy and a friend] had 56% of saves in extra man, your percentage was 55%." To me at least, that was akin to saying 'Peter is a better soldier because he can pull apart and reassemble his gun two seconds faster than you'. The percentages gave what was ultimately a deeply personal and political decision a veneer of objectivity. This veneer hurt almost as much as the shock and disappointment of non-selection. And it made me think.

Yes, we do swim in quantifiable data indicators but to use them as the sole basis for selection of goalkeepers is irresponsible at best and cowardly at worst (I've used this phrase before...). I can understand and appreciate the underlying desire to get rid of bias, emotions, politics and other 'soft' and largely un-measurable things that form a part of live human judgement. But even then, any coldly measurable, faceless, 'objective' indicators we like to call 'evidence' are a representation of some particular personal bias or desire they were created in mind with. Again, there is nothing inherently wrong in collecting data, up to the point of what economists would call the 'point of marginal (f)utility' where the effort of data collection outweighs the benefits of it at least. Quite the opposite - quality data can inform and greatly improve our decisions[69]. But the key word here is *inform* decisions, not drive them to a potentially ruinous end.[70]

The big difference between *data driven* and *data informed* decisions is that in making the latter, data is just another factor in making a decision. It could be a check on an intuitive hunch we have, a test of an idea, spotting of a new trend, support in interpreting why something has happened and more. In all these cases, knowing and understanding data helps but does not guide or even fully determine complex decisions like goalkeeper selection.

Just as numbers alone are an arguably poor way to select a goalkeeper so is a pure 'feeling', especially when unexamined. Zoran Kačić, fellow goalkeeper and writer of goalkeeping books in the sport of water polo, puts it like this: "We can't pick a goal-keeper on either stats or feel alone. We select goalkeepers on the basis of evidencing and knowing their qualities, the 'dossier' of which we collect through various challenges." Yes, it is very useful, and necessary, to track things like fitness levels, save percentages and so on of a goalkeeper. But it also helps to know how they respond to different pressure points, what do they do in the deciding moments, how they influence others and so many other largely empirically un-measurable things, some of them unique to each goalkeeper.

This diversity, even sometimes uniqueness of qualities raises an interesting question: Should (the competing) goalkeepers be selected using exactly the same criteria? After all, we owe this to goalkeepers in the name of procedural fairness, right? Same criteria, often expressed as a set of 'key competencies', are a good starting point to state the important things selector(s) want to see. They allow us to easily tally up, compare and then make a selection decision. They are great for basics and early levels of goalkeeper development. But they are a start.

Once the basics are mastered and both the skill sets and performance requirements expand, ticking off and rating against a list of closed and predetermined competencies starts to become problematic. We begin to miss things that may be critical to performance above and/or aside the list of things to look at. Imagine choosing a tennis player on the Davis Cup team based on their serve speed, number of winners, unforced errors and double faults. Tells us nothing about, for example, one player's ability to do something unexpected that throws the opponent to win the point when the game is in the balance. Tells us nothing about their ability to recover from what looked like a certain defeat ... I am sure you understand. Simply expanding the number of competencies to capture every conceivable point of comparison is no good either and would miss the point. I propose we build upon competencies and in addition to them start looking at goalkeeper's *capabilities*.[71]

Competencies are about responding to predictable challenges in a consistent way. Capabilities are about exercising individual freedom and skill to choose, act, or behave in a particular way in both predictable and unpredictable situations. A goalkeeper may not express their capabilities as regularly as they display their competencies but this does *not* imply they don't have them. They may not decide every single game with a logic-defying save or inspire their teammates with a crucial, sharp observation. But if I know as their coach that they are capable of it and 'have it in them' and the other goalkeeper probably doesn't, my choice becomes that much clearer ... Due to their intermittent displays and possible uniqueness, capabilities are of course a lot more difficult to spot and harder, even impossible to compare like competencies. However, they form an important addition to the whole picture of each goalkeeper, the 'dossier' of responses to challenges Zoran was talking about.

As for the 'fairness' argument mentioned earlier, I for one put fairness and ethics firmly before a result. You can quote me on that. But what if fairness in the form of ticking the same boxes for everyone may actually rob the team of that one goalkeeper with a unique but perhaps latent ability to do something that could well decide the most important game in our favour? We could also be forced to select a goalkeeper who 'ticks all the boxes' on paper across the compared categories, but has the capacity to wreak havoc within the group like no one else? All in the name of procedural fairness! The fairness we owe to goalkeepers doesn't lie simply in ticking the same boxes for each of them. It lies in demonstrating the *same level of effort and rigour* in spotting and scrutiny of each goalkeeper's competencies and capabilities before making a judgement without fear or favour. In this process, we also need to recognise and prosecute (not ignore and pretend they don't exist) our own preferences and bias because they are the lenses through which we see and judge goalkeepers through.

At this point I can hear some of you saying "but trying to account for every little thing about each goalkeeper is a recipe for disaster! Just how big should our 'dossier' on each goalkeeper be then?" Well, as big as it needs to be to make a decision we can justify to anyone who asks and sleep well at night after it. The greater the stakes and importance of the decision the greater the effort required in making it. As discussed in chapter 9, this

'importance' is in the eyes of the beholder and does not necessarily and/or automatically match either age group or level of
competition. But let's agree that a decision to select the senior
goalkeeper to represent their country at the World Cup needs
a far greater 'dossier' of evidence, level of scrutiny and quality
of justification than perhaps selection of a junior into the U11
development squad (never mind some self-entitled and hyper-
vigilant parents who think the opposite).

At the lowest age and competition levels, a brief but honest
and personal(ised) explanation regarding a goalkeeper's
(non)selection would probably be enough and appreciated.
It certainly beats merely slapping the 'in/out' list on the
changeroom noticeboard but at the same time it doesn't need
to be submitted to the International Court of Arbitration for
Sport. At the other end at the elite levels, coaches sometimes join
forces and/or employ a panel of peers to discuss their 'dossier'
with and justify their decision to. Such panels may even employ a
'devil's advocate' to do their best in beating the coach's argument
for a particular selection. Instead of hiding them, honestly airing
and interrogating thoughts, biases, preferences and motivations,
the what, how, why and whose mission (our own, goalkeeper's,
team's…) our decisions may help or damage is arguably a sound
and defensible way to select a goalkeeper. These methods may
not be as 'efficient' as a spreadsheet or a cut off qualifying time,
but they breed genuine quality and mutual respect a lot better
than hiding behind the cold, impersonal, inevitably selective but
spineless stats like certain percentages on one side, and nebu-
lous feelings and unqualified hunches on the other.

And just how do we compile our 'dossier'? How do we know what to include and exclude to avoid getting overwhelmed? There are so many ways but they all come down to one particular skill, mentioned a lot in this book - asking good, critical questions that capture the essence of both what we want to see and keep an open eye to what we may yet see. "Who is a better goalkeeper?" is a question that is better suited to a journalist writing a story than a coach making a decision. Instead, a coach at the Olympic level where the result matters most would be better off asking questions like "which one of these goalkeepers would I have in goal with two minutes to go and scores level in our most important game and why so?" On the other side, a coach picking goalkeepers to include in their junior development squad where the result is secondary to learning and establishing good habits may ask "who is talented but is also going to be a good role model for the behaviours I want to see in the group and why so?" The key to asking good questions is figuring out the priorities, then opening the eyes and mind to different ways of achieving them by different goalkeepers.

Yes, sometimes coaches *don't* have the luxury of time and experiences with a particular goalkeeper or a group of them to compile an extensive 'dossier' before selection. Sometimes they see goalkeepers only in a limited number of situations and environments (training camps, tournaments, playing a level above or below, low stakes games etc) and their picture of a goalkeeper is not as complete. Second-hand observations, discussions and a range of other information sources, if trusted of course, can certainly improve the picture when first-hand observations are not available.

Lastly, whatever the sources of information and thickness of our 'dossier', I challenge you to see the ability of a goalkeeper not as some sort of static 'essence' they have or not but as an ongoing series of events and responses that take place in different environments and circumstances. We can't honestly see and judge a goalkeeper's ability without considering the environment that in some way always shapes what they can and can't do. Just like for example a physical surface may affect a goalkeeper in doing and showing their best, so could the team dynamics, skill of defenders, injury, level of competition, demanded tactics or something else. This is *not* to unfairly excuse poor performance or unreasonably expect great performance. This is simply to interpret all observed instances as events in their own time and conditions. No, this does not reduce the complexity of the selection decision and probably does not make it faster to make that ultimate, binary 'in' or 'out' call either. It does however improve the confidence in selection decisions and reduces the risk of regretting them.

Speaking of risk, trying to completely eliminate it in an environment like team sport or specifically goalkeeping is as futile as it is potentially dangerous. From the coaches' perspective, the intent to control and account for every single little thing to establish an unassailable link between cause and effect and make a 100% perfect decision that will play out exactly as planned is ... utterly naive and childish. From the goalkeepers' perspective, playing *every* single game and making *every* single selection cut ever attempted makes them look a little suspicious and much like someone who has played it ultra safe without a serious push or try in their career. You can enter your own favourite quote on the benefits of risk here.

We are not robots but human beings, dealing with fellow human beings who are interacting with other human beings, with all of us making choices in the process. This creates imperfections that may and do frustrate at times but often add new challenges and produce new, creative ways of doing things in goalkeeping, sport and life.

This is of course a piece of cold comfort to a goalkeeper warming up the bench or even missing out the cut but risk *is* the actual essence, the *point* of sport. It is not something to be completely eliminated but not something to be sought for its own sake without securing some sort of return either. Whether you are looking for the next goalkeeper or making a choice between goalkeepers, risk is something very worthy to embrace and get comfortable with managing.

Because human beings are definitely not the same as human doings.

'Many Sports, Many Jobs – One Love' by Sebastian Lasic

11

Summary

"The man who grasps principles can successfully handle his own methods. The man who tries methods, ignoring principles, is sure to have trouble."

Harrington Emerson

I am sure the above would equally apply to a woman.

If you have skipped the rest of the book to read this chapter, you may be someone who wants to get 'straight to the point' and read it like a coaching manual you are perhaps used to reading. That's perfectly fine of course except this is not exactly a coaching manual. The book's guiding question "what is similar to goalkeepers across different sports?" is simply too broad to address the specifics of training and keeping goals in your chosen sport. If you are here to get the latest drills and tips - there are none, sorry. All I offer is a strong suggestion that before launching into the specific methods of 'what' and 'how' of working with goalkeepers, you honestly examine the 'why', the underlying principles and reasons for using those methods with an open mind. This 'open mind' stance may even include things done in different sports and is a chance to learn from and with each other. Why? To develop goalkeepers and goalkeeping as a unique role in sport.

A few years ago, Ratko Rudić[72], definitely water polo's if not the sport's[73] most successful coach in history and someone I had the honour of being coached by and knowing since my formative years in former Yugoslavia, toured Australia and gave a series of well-attended talks for coaches. One evening over dinner he said: "I love working with coaches here but I often get asked for 'tips' and shortcuts for various things. It took me ten years to really work out just the legwork and I'm still learning. I can give people tips but I am not sure how useful they will be with what they know." His point was that giving information in catchy chunks may be handy but ultimately of limited use without the (deeper) knowledge that builds over time and reflection. Hopefully this book helps this process in some way.

Throughout the book I generally refrain from detailed prescription of 'what works' because "everything works somewhere, nothing works everywhere. It is the context that matters the most."[74] This was Dylan William's take of the fast-proliferating, increasingly obsessive and even hostile field of 'what works' in education, my own most substantive professional field. In researching and writing this book I realised the same sobering and in many ways humbling principle can be applied to working with goalkeepers too. While I certainly *do* have my own preferred and defensible methods, I am not here to tell you what you should do. You have to work it out yourself because you know yourself, your sport, your context and, as a coach, the goalkeepers your work with better than I ever could.

This chapter is organised a set of key questions. In my view and the view of many coaches and goalkeepers from different sports with a goalkeeper I have interacted with in writing this book, these questions are useful, perhaps even essential to ask when working with goalkeepers. The answers are simply summaries of the chapters in the book. The chapters expand on these points and offer further explanation, justification, links to research, studies, quotes and examples. Feel free to dip (back) into the book anytime.

How important is the role of a goalkeeper, how it continues to change and what does 'being a goalkeeper' mean? (Chapter 2)

When you step in front of those sticks and the net to protect them, you are joining a family. An old, vast and incredibly diverse one but still a family of goalkeepers not just in the sport you happen to play but with any sport with a goalkeeper. Like it or not, know it or not, but what is expected of you as a goalkeeper now has been shaped by what those thousands of brothers and sisters have done in goals before you. At the same time, you shape the present and future of goalkeeping, deliberately or not.

The role of a goalkeeper has been traced back to ancient games and times. Through a combination of changes of rules, attitudes, trailblazing innovations and individual performances, the 'goalkeeper' has evolved from a lonely, often brutalised and one-dimensional shot-stopper on the last line of defence to what is increasingly a multi-skilled athlete that still stops the shots but now also runs defences, initiates attacks, travels up the field, shoots even, communicates and leads. Sure, the goalkeeper is still the ultimate denier or 'killjoy' as the poet Simon Armitage would put it. However, seeing that as *all* there is to goalkeeping is a pretty narrow, deficit view of it. Instead, I propose to see the goalkeeper as the builder of a team. The quality of the goalkeeper is of huge importance in any modern game with one. Statistics, insights and anecdotes, from personal to those shared by those who contributed to the book confirm the observation that a successful team with a poor goalkeeper really is a rare sporting anomaly.

There is a big difference between 'playing in goals' and 'being a goalkeeper'. The former is a playing position, the latter a part of our identity, the story of who we are as a person we tell ourselves and others. The levels of care and importance about all aspects of goalkeeping, from technical to mental to personal, are affected by how important 'being a goalkeeper' is to that person at that point in their life.

The more important this part of identity is, the more likely the goalkeeper will work harder and invest in it. This is particularly important from the coaching perspective. Not working much with goalkeepers or even ignoring them may not only be tactically or developmentally unwise. It could also be seen as not caring about the person or persons for whom being a goalkeeper is an important part of who they are at the time.

Every person, every goalkeeper is different. For all the science and its immutable laws, we all paint our own and unique goalkeeping canvas, like an artist. But knowing even the most basic science of goalkeeping and considering the underlying premises of various training approaches stands a greater chance of success than either blindly launching into working with goalkeepers or, worse, ignoring them all together. In the next chapter, we start to unpack this basic science that the art of (good) goalkeeping rests upon.

What are the fundamentals of goalkeepers' movement in any sport with one? (Chapter 3)

Goalkeeping may look simple (so does golf…) but it is a highly technical activity. Any technical work arguably starts from the most rudimentary understanding of the basics of movement in protecting the goalmouth. There are certain axioms of positioning and movement that look and feel like breathing air when applied and ridiculous when ignored. Sadly, because of this obviousness they sometimes don't get taught and /or trained. It is just assumed that, for example, the goalkeepers will work out how to cover an ideal angle, get into an optimal basic 'poise' to stand and act from, enact an efficient way to move across goals and pay attention to their centre of gravity. I have had (too) many goalkeepers in their late teens and older come up to me to thank me for showing them and explaining some of the most fundamental principles of standing, balance and moving across goals that made their job suddenly so much easier: "I never knew that!" It's not that they weren't doing aspects of it already by copying other goalkeepers. However, learning *why* it is a good idea to stand or move in a certain way was an eye opener for many.

Travelling on an arc, perpendicularly squaring the shooter, splitting the shooting angle and prioritising the near post, judicious travelling forward to reduce the 'shooting window' or backward to secure extra time to reach the shot are the axioms of movement across all sports with a goalkeeper. Under or over-covering an angle, exposure to a lob in some sports, reduced ability to effectively block, save or steal when stuck in 'no man's land' are just the most common and often very costly, even embarrassing forms of ignoring these axioms.

One of the keys to understanding coverage and movement in goals in any sport is to understand the concept of centre of gravity (COG). This is the top of an imaginary pin we could perfectly balance a goalkeeper on and from which they could travel in any direction with the least amount of effort. Keeping the COG close to the centre of the body to react from is the key reason why goalkeepers move mostly and best with small, fast and light movements instead of risking overbalancing to one side that is difficult to recover from. Speaking of movements, cat-like agility, a combination of reflexes, coordination, balance, speed, and (appropriate) response to the changing situation, is often stated as one of the key qualities of a goalkeeper. Agility is prized indeed but can be of little use if the goalkeeper is not able to 'read' the game to appear in the right place at the right time. This lies at the heart of the next key question.

What do goalkeepers do to 'read the game', anticipate and respond to be in the right place and the right time? (Chapter 4)

No matter what the sport, understanding of the basics of angles and movement is greatly complemented by the skill of 'reading the game' – appropriate and timely anticipation, preparation and execution of a move by a goalkeeper. This allows them to be at the right place at the right time to save, block, steal or distribute the ball.

Watching and tracking the ball is of course essential but there are different ways of doing that. Research by Vickers demonstrates how expert goalkeepers 'lock' their gaze on the ball earlier and for longer than novices whose eyes tend to dart around.

Speeds of basic human reaction have remained the same for millions of years and do not differ much between highly skilled athletes and untrained individuals. However, the expertise in anticipating and making decisions on what to do in the very limited time available is what makes the seemingly impossible actions quite normal and expected by goalkeepers. What makes them normal and expected is the searing into the 'small brain', the cerebellum. This is particularly important to note as shot speeds in many sports seem to be increasing due to the combination of biomechanical and physical abilities of shooters, helped by, in some sports, development of the equipment and rule changes that make faster and trickier shots possible.

Ball focus, anticipation and pattern recognition all become easier, richer and seemingly natural as goalkeepers' experience (length of playing) grows into expertise (ability to play at a high standard). Visualisation, scouting and learning about the likely opposition and thinking about one's own likely responses to at least the predictable shots and situations can all enhance the expertise.

These acts don't have to be extensive and expensive to have a positive impact but they may need explicit development and encouragement by coaches. This is because they do require some effort in observation, thinking and reflection by the goalkeeper. Questions about the most likely shots and shooters in a particular game can be asked not just by the pros but by juniors too. All this serves to prepare the goalkeeper ahead as much as possible and reduce the cognitive load for the moments when deliberate cognitive function is an impediment to the fast and almost instinctive re-action.

What are the physical demands of goalkeeping? (Chapter 5)

Regardless of the sport, goalkeepers need three key physical attributes. They need to be able to move fast, generate and sustain maximal efforts in short stints and have a solid aerobic base. What is particularly prized in goalkeepers in the physical sense is the ability to generate power to move their limbs at the fastest possible speed in the shortest amount of time. This is commonly referred to as 'speed', technically termed 'explosive power', a concept unpacked in the chapter.

Goalkeepers use the same energy systems as the field players but in very different ratios. They use the quickly replenishable phosphate energy system for short bursts up to ten seconds and the lactic anaerobic system for longer maximum efforts in front of the goal. Most of the time time though, goalkeepers use the aerobic system in recovery and/or following play in the field away from them. The aim here is not make the reader an advanced physiologist but to recognise the significantly different ways goalkeepers create and use their energy compared to the field players and the implications of this for training.

As for strength training, there is a veritable ocean of methods out there. However, what has emerged from many conversations with coaches and goalkeepers in different sports is the utmost importance of agility, mentioned before, and the 'core strength' of the deep muscles wrapping around the pelvis and lower part of the spine. Strength and stability in this area not only improves goalkeeping but also reduces the potential for injury.

Technique is another area rich in approaches, methods, and with it arguments. I propose a set of guiding questions to develop technique work that takes into account goalkeeper's genetic predispositions and current attributes instead of blindly trying to model or even clone one particular style of a goalkeeper. The questions can help set up a platform for technique work that improves performance and reduces injuries.

Before, during and after such work takes place, honestly answering questions about the necessity, reasonability and proportionality of changing an aspect of technique can save a lot of time and effort in getting goalkeepers comfortable in their skin and their own unique style while not ignoring sound bio-mechanical principles.

What are the mental demands of goalkeeping? (Chapter 6)

Goalkeeping is a mentally very demanding task and even a small act can define, make or ruin not just games but entire careers. Goalkeepers in any sport hold intense focus during games with spikes of high arousal. Ideally, they get themselves in the right zone where they are not 'asleep' on one side or frantically anxious or, worse, frozen with worry on the other side. We are all different and need different levels of arousal to perform in what Hanin called Individual Zones of Optimal Functioning.

As for emotions in goalkeeping - we need them! But for emotions to work *for* and not against us we need to recognise our own helpful or 'optimal' and unhelpful or 'dysfunctional' emotional and arousal states. What is helpful or not could differ greatly between two goalkeepers in the same team, let alone a sport.

Due to the physical demands, the importance and visibility of their role and particularly the costliness of their mistakes, goalkeepers need to be able to face, eliminate and/or manage a number of fears. Fear of injury, especially in young goalkeepers, and fear of failure are just two fears explored in this book. A very common way to minimise and prevent failure is perfectionism. This is a tendency to demand and achieve high expectations of self and others in every situation. Just like anxiety that can energise us to plan and act, the high expectations under-lying perfectionism can be helpful but only when healthy and realistic. When unhealthy, they often lead to poor performance and, worse, poor overall mental health of a goalkeeper.

This is important to recognise as the demands, expectations and scrutiny of goalkeepers intensifies, particularly at higher levels of competition. This intensification is partly due to the rule changes in some sports and more generally the advent of digital technology, social media and broader perceptions of sport and 'success' in society, fuller discussion of which is beyond the scope of this book and perhaps the topic of next one.

We all like our goalkeepers confident and motivated. But these are all pretty shallow labels unless they are actually backed by goalkeepers' justifiable belief in their own ability to accomplish the task with what they have. Bandura termed such belief as *self-efficacy* and identified four sources of it, explored in the chapter. High self-efficacy is the fuel not just for good performance but also for dealing with the inevitable howlers, bad games and setbacks that every goalkeeper in any sport has, does and will have in their career. And if there is a message to heed when it comes to the mental preparedness of goalkeepers: "Know yourself and what you can and can't control."

What is goalkeepers' 'presence' and why is it important? (Chapter 7)

Being confident in one's own ability and 'knowing thyself' in managing fears and other emotions is one thing. Exuding it to your team and the opposition is another. Such a 'presence' is the topic of chapter 7. The aim of goalkeepers 'presence' is to intimidate the opposition and lift their own team. The less energy expanded to do so for optimum result the better. The best way of doing so is by consistently keeping the ball out of the net.

This is of course easier said than done. Good goalkeepers make it look easy so people assume it is.

The ability to protect the cage is greatly enhanced by good *communication* and *leadership*. These two also happen to be some of the most misunderstood, overused and misused terms going around. While there are of course similarities, every sport has its own language and commands of plays, positions, actions that have been evolved over time, and continue to do so. Learning them and mastering their meaning and use as early as possible is a definite advantage to a goalkeeper. Importantly, these calls serve not to deliver information but to *provoke* the right meaning and *trigger* the right (re)action with the minimum effort to process it. Goalkeepers must be acutely aware of this 'injection myth' when shouting instructions to the field players.

As for the type of instructions, ask field players in any sport with a goalkeeper and they are likely to tell you they want clear, consistent, loud enough and assertive rather than quiet, shy, passive or aggressive, even obnoxious calls from their goal-keeper. Good communication is also more than shouting calls. It is about knowing the game deeply, then listening and figuring out how to tactfully lift or steady your team, not just venting your own frustration or even threatening to 'beat them until morale improves'. Practising this skill cannot start early enough and ever stop.

Communication lies at the heart of leadership. More important than the application of any particular style of leadership is an understanding that leadership is not a thing but only ever exists in relation to and with others. One goalkeeper may say all the 'right' things but remain cold as a fish to their teammates while another one inspires the same group with barely a word spoken. While there is a degree of natural talent in communication and leadership, this cannot be simply left to the goalkeeper's 'personality'. Just like dives or passes, these skills *can* be practised and, most importantly, nurtured with patience and an eye on other factors such as goalkeeper's physical and emotional maturity, team dynamics, and the environment in which the goalkeeper finds themselves in.

The much desired 'presence' may seem like a given personal trait of an individual goalkeeper. However, it is up to the individual as much as up to the environment they are in to build a strong, positive presence through development of not only their goalkeeping skills but growth in their communication and leadership.

How important are idols and role models in goalkeeping? (Chapter 8)

The sporting environment a goalkeeper grows up in has the power, and with it the responsibility, to produce second-hand, vicarious experiences. These are one of the most powerful sources of self-efficacy mentioned earlier. Numerous and high quality role models we watch and interact with and even perhaps the more remote idols we aspire to be like one day don't of course guarantee success. However, they do improve the chances of bringing up a goalkeeper who is keen to learn and aspires to improve. It could be someone's technique, bravery, intelligence, ways of dealing with things ... we like it, so we try to copy what we see.

In the question above, I distinguish between idols and role models. Idols are often remote, many levels above the goalkeeper's standard, seemingly infallible, doing things we aspire or dream of doing one day. Role models are closer to us, we often interact with them and look up to as they do something we see we could realistically do ourselves, mostly now and in the not so distant future. Of course, this distinction is not exact and the people we look up to, emulate and copy can vary anywhere in between those end-points for different reasons and aspects of goalkeeping. That's OK and it is much like having dreams and goals. Dreams are remote, hoped for but we are hardly in control of them. Goals are the achievable, sometimes daily aspirations we can do or at least realistically see ourselves doing and achieving if we put in the necessary work. We need both.

It is great, essential even, to have idols and role models but the key is not to copy or clone but borrow the parts that suit the goalkeeper's age, physical build and individual experience. Like it or not, we are also always role models (perhaps even idols!) to someone else. While we certainly can do many things to be a positive influence on others, the choice to be a role model to some is not ours to make. Just ask the NBA legend Charles Barkley, mentioned in the chapter. While someone to look up to in your own sport can be a powerful thing, looking at goalkeepers and what they do and how they overcome similar challenges in other sports may be very insightful too.

How do goalkeepers learn best? (Ch 8)

As a professional educator over the past couple of decades, I simply could not skip this question. Learning is often seen (merely) as a natural process of input and performance the output of it. This may be a crudely acceptable view but I argue it is a very impoverished one. 'Learning' is not just a naturally occurring phenomenon but a judgement about change.

Learning includes, even requires, making mistakes, but at different times, different volume and for different reasons during phases of goalkeeper's development. We see mistakes in learning and performing through two lenses. The lens of importance is a mixture of our own, internal expectations and the external expectations of those around us. Perceived importance can lead anywhere from a perfect unison of shared purpose within a team on one side to cheating and similar ugly scenes on the other. The other lens we see mistakes through is the lens of competence. I use the four stage 'conscious competence' model to trace the development of a goalkeeper from unconscious incompetence as a beginner to unconscious competence as an expert. This is to help understand the concept of competence and with it (the importance of) mistakes.

Ever wondered why goalkeepers regularly seem to end up coaching and working with goalkeepers? I wrestle with this question with some important caveats about the importance of constantly recognising goalkeeper's needs before blindly adopting coach's' own views, styles and methods used in the past. Game, rules, people and environments change and coaches need to adjust, grow and learn too!

While there is arguably no single best way to bring up a goalkeeper, a sensible progress from initially telling to gradually empowering a goalkeeper towards a partnership and shared responsibility for coaching is an approach that breeds trust and with it results. I argue that asking 'what is the best way to bring up a goalkeeper?' may lead to potentially very frustrating flipping from one method to another. I propose it may be better to ask 'what matters?' first and along the way as things change. In the chapter, I offer some guiding sub-questions that may frame the responses. Whatever the responses though, they need to have a key ingredient in bringing up a goalkeeper - patience.

How to find and select a goalkeeper? (Ch 9)

In writing this book I asked dozens of goalkeepers from different sports how they started goalkeeping. By far the most common responses, including mine, can be summarised as 'happy accidents', the impossibly-planned-for love affairs. It reminded me of a statement by an old wise coach about the priority of this love that stayed with me for thirty years of working with particularly young people.

When searching for our (next) goalkeeper, we can certainly look for a good athlete with the necessary physical and mental makeup, their history and likely trajectory. Doing so however, we need to be careful to consider different development and maturation rates, especially with early specialisation and overload that may on one side blossom and possibly kill the love of goalkeeping on the other.

The explosion of ways to collect various numerical, quantifiable data has fuelled a dangerous propensity to make data driven instead of data informed decisions in selecting goalkeepers. I use the word dangerous because using quantifiable data to *drive* decisions alone makes it easy to lose sight of what we are after. In making data *informed* decisions though, data is just another factor in making what are ultimately subjective, but responsible and justifiable decisions. Ideally, such decisions would be based on a balanced 'dossier' of each goalkeeper that includes a mixture of quantifiable data and unavoidable personal observations, feelings and preferences in selecting one particular goalkeeper ahead of another.

Another growing tendency is to represent a goalkeeper as a set of competencies to rate them by. While this can be useful, I propose building on competencies to also consider goalkeeper's capabilities. They are the unique, hard to compare, individual and often less frequently visible qualities that a decent 'dossier' cannot go without. Just how extensive such a dossier should be in making a selection decision depends on the context of the decision, an issue discussed in the chapter.

Ultimately, the necessary imperfections of human decisions create a risk of things not always going to one's preferences. But this I argue is the *essence* of sport, of innovation and development. Embrace it!

'Connect' by Sebastian Lasic

Next step

If there is something that has become even clearer in writing this book it is this - yes, we play different sports but we share so much as goalkeepers. Hopefully you now have a similar sense of it too.

Pressures of time, performance and maybe lack of contacts with goalkeepers and coaches in other sports often force us to focus only on what we know and can see in our own sport. Reaching out of our own sporting silos may just give us that edge we seek and at the same time unite us in developing the beautiful art and science of goalkeeping.

You would be surprised what a water polo goalkeeper can learn from hockey, a coach in lacrosse from a colleague in futsal, or a young football goalkeeper from a mentor playing handball and more. This is sometimes a simple phone call, an email, a link, a post, a conversation away. I encourage you to start it, at least.

Feel free to connect via theloveofgoalkeeping.net website, Facebook, Instagram (@theloveofgoalkeeping), Twitter (@theloveofGK) or you can send me a simple email at tomaz@theloveofgoalkeeping.net. I would love to hear your thoughts about the book or things to do with goalkeeping, no matter what the sports your play.

Speaking of the website, theloveofgoalkeeping.net contains a growing set of resources and interactive content that supports and expands the topics discussed in the book. You are very welcome to visit and share.

Over to you... yours in goals

Tomaž

About the author

I fell in love with goalkeeping when I was ten years old in my hometown club Triglav in Kranj, Slovenia. Since then, I played for several clubs, most notably Mladost from Zagreb, Croatia, with whom I won several national titles and two European Champions League titles in water polo. After migrating to Australia in the early 1990s, I won several national titles with Fremantle Mariners. Between 1984 and 2000, I played for (now former) Yugoslavia, Slovenia and Australia at the highest international level. I coached Australian National Water

Polo League teams, worked as the Head Coach of Womens Water Polo Programme at Western Australian Institute of Sport, and assisted several male and female Australian Olympic Water Polo Teams and individuals with specialist goalkeeping coaching.

I have a Bachelor and Masters research degree in education, my current professional field. Over the past two decades I have worked as a humanities and design teacher in some of the most socioeconomically disadvantaged high schools, a researcher and writer in the sociology of education, and an educational coach and mentor to fellow teachers.

I live and work in Perth, Western Australia, always keen and curious to hear from people around the world. You can get easily in touch with me via The Love of Goalkeeping or personal social media accounts.

Notes

Chapter 1 - Introduction

[1] An official 'goalkeeper' position exists in (ordered alphabetically) bandy, beach football, camogie, field hockey, Gaelic football, hurling, international rules football, floorball, football, futsal, handball, ice hockey, lacrosse, ringette, rinkball, rink bandy, roller hockey, shinty and water polo.

In this book, football is the generic name used for 'association football', also called soccer in some English speaking cultures, the world's biggest sport in terms of participation and revenue.

Jones M, "Ospina - Why I Love Being a Keeper" <https://www.arsenal.com/news/ospina-why-i-love-being-goalkeeper> accessed April 2, 2020

Hodgson T, "The Love of Goalkeeping" <https://www.a-love-supreme.com/post/2019/07/16/the-love-of-goalkeeping> accessed April 10, 2020

"Trailblazer Ashleigh Johnson Takes Water Polo Into Uncharted Waters" <https://www.olympic.org/news/trailblazer-ashleigh-johnson-takes-water-polo-into-uncharted-waters> accessed April 2, 2020

Ioannou-Marsh I, "Goalkeeping 101: On Learning to Love the Undesired Position" <https://www.theroar.com.au/2018/07/28/goalkeeping-101-learning-love-undesired-position/> accessed April 2, 2020

Just a few recent and high profile declarations of such a love.

Chapter 2 – The role and importance of a goalkeeper

[3] Armitage S, "World Cup 2010: Why I Love Goalkeepers" *The Guardian* (June 15, 2010) <https://www.theguardian.com/global/2010/jun/15/simon-armitage-goalkeepers> accessed November 3, 2019

4 You will find a treasure trove of historical books on goalkeeping in football in Jonathan Wilson's book The Outsider: A History of the Goalkeeper, referenced below.

5 "5 Things You Didn't Know About The History of Goalkeeping" (*Renegade GK,* August 18, 2010) <https://renegade-gk.com/blogs/the-renegade/5-things-you-didnt-know-about-the-history-of-goalkeeping> accessed November 5, 2019

6 Jonathan Wilson *The Outsider; A History of the Goalkeeper* (Hatchette 2012) accessed 25 September 2019

7 Marindin GE, "The Game of 'Harpastum' or 'Pheninda.'" (1890) 4 *The Classical Review* 145

8 "Lev Yashin" (*Wikipedia,* March 14, 2020) <https://en.wikipedia.org/wiki/Lev_Yashin> accessed April 10, 2019

9 Nabokov, Vladimir, *Speak, Memory* (Weidenfeld and Nicolson, 1966)

10 McCann A and Fischer-Baum R, "Which Olympic Sport Is Hardest On Its Goalies?" <https://fivethirtyeight.com/features/which-olympic-sport-is-hardest-on-its-goalies/> accessed October 2, 2019

11 Wilson C, "Guide to Water Polo Goalkeeping" (*Guide to water polo goalkeeping*) <https://www.thewaterpologoalie.com/wp-content/uploads/2016/03/Craig_Wilsons_Goalkeeping_Guide.pdf> accessed September 2, 2019

12 Tighe S, "The Evolution of the Goalkeeper: What Makes the Perfect Modern-Day No. 1?" (*Bleacher Report*November 6, 2018) <https://bleacherreport.com/articles/2802528-the-evolution-of-the-goalkeeper> accessed January 2, 2020

Chapter 3 – Moving like a cat

13 Peet M, *Keeper* (Candlewick Press 2007)

14 "Centre of Gravity" (*Physiopedia*) <https://www.physio-pedia.com/Centre_of_Gravity> accessed December 10, 2019

15 Quinn E, "VeryWell Fit" <https://www.verywellfit.com/understand-ing-agility-in-sports-3120338> accessed November 22, 2019

Chapter 4 – Reading the game

[16] Kwon K-A and others, "High-Speed Camera Characterization of Voluntary Eye Blinking Kinematics" (2013) 10 Journal of The Royal Society Interface 20130227 <https://www.ncbi.nlm.nih.gov/pmc/articles/PMC4043155/>

[17] "Laws Of Movement Learning And Control - IResearchNet" (*Laws Of Movement Learning And Control*February 24, 2017) <https://psychology.iresearchnet.com/sports-psychology/motor-development/laws-of-movement-learning-and-control/> accessed January 22, 2020

[18] Obetko M, Babic M and Peraček P, "Changes in Disjunctive Reaction Time of Soccer Goalkeepers in Selected Training Load Zones" (2019) 19 Journal of Physical Education and Sport 420 <https://www.researchgate.net/publication/331558470_Changes_in_disjunctive_reaction_time_of_soccer_goalkeepers_in_selected_training_load_zones>

[19] The table is based on adult males and their fastest recorded shot speeds. The values would need to be adjusted for adult females and juniors. 'Fast' shots are 80% and 'Average' shots 60% of the fastest values. The 'common' and 'long' are approximate distances for shots in that sport.

[20] Robson D, "Why Athletes Need a 'Quiet Eye'" <https://www.bbc.com/future/article/20180627-is-quiet-eye-the-secret-to-success-for-athletes> accessed December 6, 2019

[21] Vickers JN, "The Quiet Eye: Reply to Sixteen Commentaries" (2016) 2016 Current Issues in Sport Science (CISS) <http://www.visualcognition.ca/spering/publications/Spering.Schuetz.CISS.2016.pdf>

[22] Vickers JN, *Perception, Cognition, and Decision Training: the Quiet Eye in Action* (Human Kinetics 2007)

[23] Can You Train to Read Your Opponent's Mind? NeuroTracker <https://neurotracker.net/2018/04/05/can-train-read-opponents-mind> accessed July 28, 2020

[24] Libet B and others, "Time Of Conscious Intention To Act In Relation To Onset Of Cerebral Activity (Readiness-Potential)" (1983) 106 Brain 623

[25] Fifel K, "Readiness Potential and Neuronal Determinism: New Insights on Libet Experiment" (2018) 38 The Journal of Neuroscience 784

[26] Trafton A, "In the Blink of an Eye" <http://news.mit.edu/2014/in-the-blink-of-an-eye-0116> accessed January 22, 2020

[27] Ghose T, "'Muscle Memory' May Not Really Exist" <https://www.livescience.com/56218-muscles-have-no-strength-memory.html> accessed February 3, 2020

[28] Bergland C, "How Does Practice Hardwire Long-Term Muscle Memory?" <https://www.psychologytoday.com/intl/blog/the-athletes-way/201503/how-does-practice-hardwire-long-term-muscle-memory> accessed January 13, 2020

[29] Bergland C, "No. 1 Reason Practice Makes Perfect" <https://www.psychologytoday.com/intl/blog/the-athletes-way/201110/no-1-reason-practice-makes-perfect> accessed February 4, 2020

Chapter 5 – Fit and able

[30] Pyke FS, *Better Coaching: Advanced Coach's Manual* (Australian Sports Commission 2001) Please note that most of the references in this chapter come from this excellent and highly reputable source among Australian coaches and beyond.

[31] Valle C, "Explosive Strength Development: Myths, Methodology, and Measurement" <https://simplifaster.com/articles/explosive-strength-development/> accessed January 21, 2020

[32] Ireland A, "What Exercise Does to Your Bones" <https://theconversation.com/what-exercise-does-to-your-bones-57524> accessed November 19, 2019

[33] The recently released documentary 'The Last Dance' shows how the coach of Chicago Bulls and a few expert commentators and former players in the mid 1980s commented on the freshly drafted Michael Jordan's lack of height along the lines of "it's a shame he is not 7 foot tall". Knowing what Jordan achieved since, it's a perfect example of a useless lament about (the lack of) genetic attributes.

34 Di Salvo V and others, "Activity Profile of Elite Goalkeepers during Football Match-Play" (2008) 48 Journal of Sports Medicine and Fitness 443 <https://www.ncbi.nlm.nih.gov/pubmed/18997646>

Please note that this is just one study, and often quoted, in football alone. Similar studies of movement and energy expenditure have been done in many other sports, many of them looked at but not quoted in here. This book is does not contain and an extensive academic literature review in any, let alone across different sports. If such cross-sports review exists or is being planned, the author would love to hear from you.

Chapter 6 – Inside goalkeeper's head

35 Reng, Ronald, *A Life Too Short: The Tragedy of Robert Enke* (Yellow Jersey, 2011)

This is actually Reng's second book on the topic of goalkeepers. His 2004 book "The Keeper of Dreams: One Man's Controversial Story of Life in the English Premiership" tells a personal story of a talented goalkeeper Lars Leese plucked from relative obscurity to the English Premier League, his rise and struggles.

36 Ruiz M, Raglin J and Hanin Y, "The Individual Zones of Optimal Functioning (IZOF) Model (1978–2014): Historical Overview of Its Development and Use" (2015) 15 International Journal of Sport and Exercise Psychology <https://www.tandfonline.com/doi/abs/10.1080/1612197X.2015.1041545?journalCode=rijs20> accessed January 15, 2020

37 "Individual Zones of Optimal Functioning (IZOF)" (*Sportlyzer Academy*) <https://academy.sportlyzer.com/wiki/arousal-and-performance/individual-zones-of-optimal-functioning-izof/> accessed March 12, 2020

38 Bar-Eli M, "In the Zone: How Balancing Stress Levels Improves Performance [Excerpt]" <https://blog.oup.com/2017/11/balancing-stress-levels-improves-performance/> accessed January 7, 2020

39 Ford JL and others, "Sport-Related Anxiety: Current Insights" (2017) 8 Open Access Journal of Sports Medicine 205 <https://www.ncbi.nlm.nih.gov/pmc/articles/PMC5667788/#!po=10.0000> accessed February 3, 2020

40 Heshmat S, "Anxiety vs. Fear: What Is the Difference?" <https://www.psychologytoday.com/au/blog/science-choice/201812/anxiety-vs-fear> accessed January 20, 2020

41 Zhang S, Woodman T and Roberts R, "Anxiety and Fear in Sport and Performance," *Oxford Research Encyclopedia of Psychology* (Oxford University Press 2018) <https://www.researchgate.net/publication/329881672_Anxiety_and_Fear_in_Sport_and_Performance> accessed January 12, 2020 A great resource to explore further, full text available online.

42 Berlin L, "Irish Hurling: The Ball Moves 100 Miles per Hour. So Why Don't Goalkeepers Want to Wear Facemasks?" (*Slate Magazine*April 13, 2011) <https://slate.com/culture/2011/04/irish-hurling-the-ball-moves-100-miles-per-hour-so-why-don-t-goalkeepers-want-to-wear-facemasks.html> accessed December 16, 2019

43 Kelly A, "Is Pressure in Sports a Myth?" <http://www.sportpsychologytoday.com/sport-psychology-for-coaches/is-pressure-a-myth/> accessed December 10, 2019

44 Nash C, "The Loneliness of the Sub Goalkeeper" *The Guardian* (March 9, 2018) <https://www.theguardian.com/football/the-set-pieces-blog/2018/mar/08/loneliness-substitute-goalkeeper> accessed December 4, 2019

45 pg. 200, Jonathan Wilson *The Outsider; A History of the Goalkeeper* (Hatchette 2012)

46 Bandura A, "Self-Efficacy: Toward a Unifying Theory of Behavioral Change." (1977) 84 Psychological Review 191

47 Head R, "Self-Efficacy and Sports Performance" <http://www.sportpsychologytoday.com/youth-sports-psychology/self-efficacy-and-sports-performance/> accessed February 2, 2020

48 Ogden M, "Goalkeepers Go to 'Dark Places' after Making a High-Profile Mistake. How Do the Pros Handle the Pressure?" <https://www.espn.com/soccer/english-premier-league/23/blog/post/3845064/goalkeepers-go-to-dark-places-after-making-a-high-profile-mistake-how-do-the-pros-handle-the-pressure> accessed November 20, 2019

[49] A wonderful example from tennis and Ash Barty, world's best female player in 2019:

Smith A and Kelsey-Sugg A, "Ash Barty's Mentor Helped Her Soar in Tennis and in Life — and His Advice Can Help You Too" <https://www.abc.net.au/news/2019-11-15/ash-barty-mentor-ben-crowe-advice-for-on-and-off-sports-field/11704022> accessed November 20, 2019

Chapter 7 – The Presence

[50] Kamp JVD and Masters RSW, "The Human Müller-Lyer Illusion in Goalkeeping" (2008) 37 Perception 951

[51] Schaap R, "Playing On The Edge: The Psychology Of A Goalkeeper" <https://www.npr.org/sections/showmey-ourcleats/2010/06/30/128222244/playing-on-the-edge-the-psychology-of-a-goal-keeper> accessed January 5, 2020

[52] McKay H, *Why Don't People Listen* (Macmillan Australia 1994)

[53] I borrow many insights on the interplay of the individual and environment from the literature on teacher agency, explored in Priestley M, Biesta GJJ and Robinson S, *Teacher Agency: an Ecological Approach* (Bloomsbury Academic 2019). Their work builds on the original 'ecological' view of human agency (not just in teaching context), first proposed by Emirbayer and Mische in the 1990's.

Chapter 8 – Idols and role models

[54] "Guy McKenna" (Wikipedia, 10 February, 2020) <https://en.wikipedia.org/wiki/Guy_McKenna>

[55] Biskup C and Pfister G, "I Would Like to Be Like Her/Him: Are Athletes Role-Models for Boys and Girls?" (1999) 5 European Physical Education Review 199 <https://journals.sagepub.com/doi/pdf/10.1177/1356336X990053003>

[56] *Nike Air Commercial Charles Barkley* <https://youtu.be/NNOdFJAG3pE>

[57] Resnick S, "Athletes Are Not Role Models, But They Can Be Idols" <https://bleacherreport.com/articles/226238-athletes-are-not-role-models-but-they-can-be-idols> accessed January 13, 2020

58 Levine S, "Our Illusions of Role Models, Heroes, and Idols; Idols Who Inspire and Reassure Us Are Ordinary People, Both Worthy and Flawed." <https://www.psychologytoday.com/au/blog/our-emo-tional-footprint/201712/our-illusions-role-models-heroes-and-idols> accessed February 1, 2020

Chapter 9 – Teaching and learning the craft

59 p.6, Biesta GJJ, *The Beautiful Risk of Education* (Routledge 2016)

60 Randy Glasbergen, Cartoon No. 2036. Image used with the permission of the author's estate.

61 "Four Stages of Competence" (*Wikipedia*April 5, 2020) <https://en.wiki-pedia.org/wiki/Four_stages_of_competence> accessed February 10, 2020

62 "Tacit Knowledge" (*Wikipedia*March 24, 2020) <https://en.wikipedia.org/wiki/Tacit_knowledge> accessed April 13, 2020

63 Routledge, "Power/Knowledge" (*Social Theory Rewired*) <http://rout-ledgesoc.com/category/profile-tags/powerknowledge> accessed March 10, 2020

This is but a shortest of primers in what is a deep field of fascinating sociological and philosophical thought by Michel Foucault. His ideas extend well beyond the scope of sport and offer a particular understanding of the world we live, its construction and its effects.

64 Netolicky D, "What Matters in Teaching and Learning?" <https://theeduflaneuse.com/2020/01/28/what-matters-in-teaching-and-learn-ing/> accessed February 2, 2020

65 "Self Determination Theory Overview" (*selfdeterminationtheory.org*) <https://selfdeterminationtheory.org/theory/> accessed February 13, 2020

66 "Drive: The Surprising Truth About What Motivates Us" (*Wikipedia*November 14, 2019) <https://en.wikipedia.org/wiki/Drive:_The_Surprising_Truth_About_What_Motivates_Us> accessed February 27, 2020

[67] Upton M, "7 Principles of Non Linear Pedagogy" <https://www.play-football.com.au/news/7-principles-non-linear-pedagogy> accessed October 12, 2019

Chapter 10 – Finding and selecting a goalkeeper

[68] The 2011 film https://www.imdb.com/title/tt1210166/ starring Brad Pitt is based on the book 'Moneyball: The Art of Winning an Unfair Game' written by Michael Lewis in 2003.

[69] Yam, Derrick. "A Data Driven Goalkeeper Evaluation Framework." Sloan Sports Conference, *MIT Sloan Sports Analytics Conference*, Mar. 2019, http://www.sloansportsconference.com/wp-content/uploads/2019/02/Data-Driven-Goalkeeper-Evaluation-Framework-1.pdf.

[70] Harris M and Tayler B, "Don't Let Metrics Undermine Your Business" (*Don't Let Metrics Undermine Your Business*August 27, 2019) <https://hbr.org/2019/09/dont-let-metrics-undermine-your-business> accessed March 2, 2020

[71] Bachkirova T and Smith CL, "From Competencies to Capabilities in the Assessment and Accreditation of Coaches" (2015) 13 International Journal of Evidence Based Coaching and Mentoring 123 <https://psycnet.apa.org/record/2016-40282-009> accessed February 2, 2020

Chapter 11 - Summary

[72] "Ratko Rudic" (*International Swimming Hall of Fame*) <https://ishof.org/ratko-rudic.html> accessed March 11, 2020

[73] Robinson, J & Cohen B "The World's Greatest Coach Is Not Who You Think" (Wall Street Journal, May 19, 2020) https://www.wsj.com/articles/the-worlds-greatest-coach-is-not-who-you-think-11589882400; accessed May 22, 2020

[74] Mroz A and others, "Don't Leave Failure in the Shadows – It Can Light Your Way to Success" (*Times Education Supplement,* May 10, 2018) https://www.tes.com/news/dont-leave-failure-shadows-it-can-light-your-way-success; accessed March 23, 2020